250-104

Education for Freedom and Responsibility

Edmund Ezra Day

EDUCATION FOR FREEDOM AND RESPONSIBILITY

Selected Essays by

EDMUND EZRA DAY

Edited by Milton R. Konvitz

Essay Index Reprint Series

 BOOKS FOR LIBRARIES PRESS

FREEPORT, NEW YORK

INTERNATIONAL STANDARD BOOK NUMBER:
0-8369-2391-X

LIBRARY OF CONGRESS CATALOG CARD NUMBER:
78-142618

PRINTED IN THE UNITED STATES OF AMERICA
BY
NEW WORLD BOOK MANUFACTURING CO., INC.
HALLANDALE, FLORIDA 33009

10.00

Foreword

ANYONE who knew Edmund Ezra Day well was assured that he was a man dedicated to education. It is little wonder that he saw the world with the eyes of a teacher, for he began to teach at the age of twenty-three. He was first an instructor in economics at Dartmouth, and he continued to teach—at Harvard and the University of Michigan—for more than twenty years. During these two decades Dr. Day won distinction as a great teacher and as an economist of first rank.

His distinction as teacher and economist led him into administration, where he was provided with many opportunities for the application of his talents, always in the field of education. He was chairman of the Department of Economics at Harvard, founder and first dean of the School of Business Administration at Michigan, director of social sciences for the Rockefeller Foundation, and director of general education for the General Education Board.

At the age of fifty-three Dr. Day became the fifth president of Cornell University, in which post he served for twelve years, to be followed by a brief period as chancellor. On March 23, 1951, he died of a heart attack at the age of sixty-seven.

Although Dr. Day's best years as a teacher were spent at Harvard and Michigan, it was at Cornell that he left his most enduring mark as a great educational administrator. During his years of service the enrollment at Cornell increased from 6,300 to more than 10,000 students. Six schools were added to the University: the Graduate School of Aeronautical Engineering, the School of Business and Public Administration, the School of Chemical and Metallurgical Engineering, the School of Nursing, the School of Nutrition, and the New York State School of Industrial and Labor Relations.

The establishment of new schools and laboratories at Cornell was an implementation by Dr. Day of a basic tenet of his educational philosophy: to extend the frontiers of knowledge. For Dr. Day had no fear of ideas. Human progress, he said, "can be more surely made in the light than in darkness." When, in 1944, he was interested in the establishment of a comprehensive course of study in contemporary Russian civilization, he was attacked from various quarters. His answer to his critics reflected a profound conviction. "It is part of the respect we owe to our youth," he said, "to deny it no knowledge that will enable it to bear, as it will bear resolutely and willingly, and in the enduring tradition of freedom, the weight of the world that is descending upon its shoulders."

Dr. Day was vitally concerned with the balance between research and teaching. He did not leave it to chance to establish this balance but actively sought ways and means to make the relations between teaching and research both harmonious and productive.

He guided the affairs of Cornell through the tragic years of World War II and during the difficult postwar years—

FOREWORD

a period when it would have been easier for him to have
acquiesced, now and then, to the forces of repression and
reaction. Yet during this entire period there was not a single
instance of suppression of student opinion or of interference
with freedom of teaching or research. On the contrary,
Dr. Day firmly and unequivocally defended intellectual and
academic freedom against every attempt that was made to
suppress or weaken such freedom.

These tangible and intangible achievements will remain
through the years as enduring memorials to Dr. Day. Cornell's gratitude to him for his tangible contributions has been
expressed by naming the new administration building Edmund Ezra Day Hall. The University's gratitude for his intangible contributions, for his philosophy of education, for
his work in constantly forging links between education and
freedom, is in part expressed by sponsorship of this volume
by the Trustees of the University.

DEANE W. MALOTT

Cornell University

vii

Preface

AFTER he became president of Cornell University and assumed what President Conant calls the duties of "academical superintendence," Dr. Day seldom wrote for publication. He did, however, often prepare addresses for alumni meetings, commencements, professional groups, and meetings of teachers or school administrators. As I read through these papers, slowly the conception of the book evolved itself. While there was repetition along with a scattering of ideas and insights, there were also a consistency of theme and a recurrence of conceptions and convictions: almost everything Dr. Day said had relevance to education—its objectives and its methods. While he spoke on and for occasions, the thoughts he expressed were not "occasional," ephemeral, but came out of firm belief. This condition made it possible for me to accomplish my editorial task without feeling that I was violating any conscientious scruples. Just as Emerson could construct his essays by drawing his thoughts out of his journals, so, I felt, I could construct Dr. Day's book out of his papers: there would be nothing in the book which was not written by Dr. Day himself, but his words would be made to fit into a system of categories and an order—categories derived from the material itself, and an order organic to the thoughts themselves. The result is this book, one which, I like to think, Dr. Day himself would have wanted to see published.

The title of the book is, I think, a fair description of the book's contents, and is also an indirect acknowledgment of Dr. Day's friendship with and indebtedness to Carl Becker. To both of them, as to Jefferson, democracy was inconceivable without education—and more and more education; and the essence of democracy was freedom and responsibility. Without education, there can be no freedom and responsibility; without freedom and responsibility, there can be no education: they are all inextricably intertwined. One could, therefore, say "Education for Freedom and Responsibility" or "Education, Freedom, and Responsibility." Since the book is concerned with educational methods and objectives, I chose the former expression as closer to the direction of Dr. Day's thoughts.

M. R. K.

Cornell University

Contents

GENERAL EDUCATION

Responsibilities of General

Education in a Free Society

MY THINKING with regard to general education rests at bottom on the fundamental thesis that general education is a social function. The ultimate responsibilities of general education are social responsibilities, that is, responsibilities to society. Let no one suppose that this thesis implies an over-all political entity—a state—which may deal lightly with the lives of the individuals who live within its orbit. In America we subscribe to no such doctrine. We believe in a society which recognizes the dignity and worth of the individual and establishes the necessary conditions for his or her many-sided worth-while living; we believe in a government that establishes common justice and promotes general welfare. But these very ideals make it essential that individual interests be bent to social ends. Individuals may expect to be benefited by general education; most assuredly they are; but the advantages they obtain through general education are ultimately warranted only as they serve more than individual aims. It is quite clear that no persistent clash between individual and social advantages can be tolerated in the provision of general education in any enduring culture. Fortunately, subject to certain limitations which have to be

3

recognized, individual benefits and social advantages can be wisely and successfully fostered through general education at the same time and by the same means.

Broadly speaking, the social responsibilities of general education fall into two main categories: (1) those directed toward the maintenance of social solidarity and stability; and (2) those designed to promote social differentiation and change. The first of these broad divisions of function has to do with transmitting and perpetuating the culture, the second with adjusting and elevating it.

That transmitting and perpetuating the culture is a primary function of general education is manifested in all forms of human society from the most primitive and simple to the most advanced and complex. Human society as we know it could hardly persist did not each succeeding generation in large measure adopt the customs, habits, manners, morals, modes of thought, prejudices and preconceptions of the preceding generation. This process of social imitation is maintained, of course, by a wide variety of social agencies and forces, of which the school is only one. But the extent to which the school is made responsible for transmitting the culture is increasing rather than diminishing. It is more than ever important, therefore, that the school should see clearly what is involved concretely in the discharge of this fundamental duty.

The role of general education in modifying and elevating the culture is not as evident as is the transmission role. In general, it is safe to say that impulses making for social change have had their immediate source largely outside the school, and that the marvelous advances in science and technology which have characterized civilization of late have had little direct connection with the processes of general

4

education, at least as formally organized. Moreover, it is clear that there will always be serious restraints imposed upon any attempt by the schools openly and explicitly to change the social order. Yet, beyond question, general education in some of its phases can be a ferment from which social changes are almost certain to spring. At any rate, it is to be recognized that, whatever may be the record of the recent past, general education has important contributions to make to social progress and that certain specific objectives should be set to this end.

In this connection it should be observed that the two types of functioning for general education which have been noted —maintenance of social solidarity and stability, and promotion of social differentiation and change—are to some extent in opposition to one another. There is, hence, a fundamental problem of keeping disparate functions in appropriate co-ordination or balance. In our own times social changes have been so extensively and rapidly induced that the maintenance of social stability has become a task of huge proportions, taxing the resources of education in all its varied forms and phases. For the time being, the more pressing duties of general education relate to ways and means of effecting an adequate social solidarity. Increasingly it is becoming clear that the whole people must share common convictions, loyalties, and enthusiasms if any social order is to hold together and be efficient. The authoritarian governments of Europe demonstrate one way to meet this basic requirement. Can the great democracies, with equal pointedness, show another but profoundly different way? I believe they can if they will but apply their utmost resources to the task. The problem is one of social discipline. Unless as a people we can develop such a discipline on a voluntary

basis—unless, in other words, we can discipline ourselves—
the coercive authority of some group employing force will
impose the necessary social discipline we have failed to develop. For the time being, general education must make this
general problem of the ways and means of social solidarity
one of its prime concerns. Such social changes as are ac-
celerated should be those which conduce to that underlying
stability without which other social changes cannot possibly contribute to social progress.

These purposes of general education can best be exam-
ined in terms of specific outcomes to be sought. Five broad
types of outcome may be distinguished: (1) the acquisition
of basic skills; (2) the formation of habits; (3) the cultivation of interests, sensitivity, and appreciation; (4) the
promotion of knowledge and understanding; and (5) the
inculcation of attitudes and ideals. I shall comment briefly
on each.

(1) The most obvious responsibilities of general education relate to the mastery of certain basic skills. No one
questions, for example, the importance in the schools of the
three R's. Communication in the mother tongue is so indispensable to our culture that we take for granted the necessity of teaching all to speak, read, hear, and write it. But
the standards we set in this connection are lamentably low.
In regard to oral use of language the schools do little; the
job is supposed to have been completed before the children
come to school. Neither in speaking nor in listening do most
schools undertake seriously to cultivate greater skill. Teaching to read, on the other hand, looms as the largest single
assignment of the early grades. While results upon the whole
are gratifying, much more could be done to cultivate reading
with understanding. Writing gets attention, but attention in

6

many schools inadequately or ineffectually given. So far as simple handwriting is concerned, the outcomes appear to be generally satisfactory. But writing as a means of lucid self-expression remains for most an unknown art. In general, it can be said that much still remains to be done to discharge fully the responsibilities of general education with respect to those skills which involve the use of the mother tongue in both the oral and the written forms. Educational experimentation and innovation, whatever their promise in other directions, should not be permitted to obstruct the progress that needs so much to be made in teaching our youth how to use more satisfactorily the language in which our culture communicates.

Another basic skill that clearly has to be mastered by all has to do with the elementary arithmetical operations. Numerical concepts, quantitative relationships, units of measurement, and arithmetical processes permeate our day-to-day existence. General education must see that all learn how to deal with them in their simpler forms. This does not imply an extended course of rigorous mathematical training, even of an elementary sort; it does imply sustained instruction on how arithmetical operations are to be applied in concrete situations. To a surprising extent the mathematical training now included in general education fails to give social competence; it should be made to do so.

To the extent of the individual's capacity, general education must concern itself with the cultivation and exercise of intellectual power. While much lip-service is paid in educational circles to the importance of intellectual growth through education, actual school practices, especially in days of wide educational experimentation, are ofttimes distressingly weak in their service to that end.

7

A part of the present deficiency appears to stem from what may be called the data complex. Informational outcomes of instruction are badly overrated; data returned to the instructor intact, one might almost say in the original wrapping unopened, are assumed to have been in some mysterious way profitably assimilated. Power to remember and to repeat is often all that is requisite to successful completion of the work.

It is, of course, fairly obvious that this type of experience bears only indirectly, and not always significantly, on the development of intellectual power. Not that memory is to be regarded as of no educational consequence, or knowledge as an educational impediment. There is not the conflict between knowing and thinking that some statements would lead one to infer. No one has yet succeeded in demonstrating that constructive thinking can take place in a factual vacuum. But at times thought does get mired in an ooze of unorganized facts; and research, lost in a forest of trivial data. What is especially needed in the cultivation of intellectual power is repeated and varied experience in the critical analysis of manageable material, in the formulation of appropriate inferences, in the interpretation of data, in the organization of material, in the solving of problems. Standards of accuracy have to be evolved and applied. The processes of thought and expression have to be disciplined through exercise in the principles of grammar, rhetoric, and logic, with a view to expressing thought in words and ordering thoughts in logical form. The nature of proof and of induction and deduction have to be learned from concrete cases. Growth of intellectual power, particularly in its constructive and creative phases, is far from a simple and easy achievement; it requires most careful training and sustained and

8

rigorous effort. In general, our schools are failing to bring it about in anything like the measure they should.

Intellectual power is no social panacea; not too much should be expected of it; but the fact remains that in the long run the exercise of intellectual power is at the same time one of the surest sources of human satisfaction and one of the indispensable bases of social progress. In so far as we retain an abiding faith in intelligence, the cultivation of intellectual power must remain one of general education's primary responsibilities.

Beyond the skills displayed in using the mother tongue lie certain skills involving the employment of non-verbal forms of expression. Ability to use these diverse art forms is of great significance if civilization is to be ennobled and life enriched. The esthetic capacity which lies dormant in a host of people, young and old, is only now coming to be recognized. Progressive education has amply demonstrated that impressive results are to be had in this area. General education should do much more than it has done to discover and develop skill in non-verbal expression in all its diverse and intriguing forms.

General education may also wisely acknowledge responsibility for the development of certain sensory and motor functions to a higher level of efficiency. Thus visual discrimination can be sharpened, tactile sensitivity heightened, manual dexterity increased, bodily co-ordination improved in ways that are bound ultimately to prove fruitful. The immediate educational results from such training may not be evident, but by and large the more general education can be directed toward the mastery of general skills, as contrasted with purely formal informational outcomes, the more permanent and substantial are likely to be its effects. This

9

is especially true, of course, in the earlier stages of general education, when students are still in the highly formative stages of individual development.

(2) The second group of responsibilities of general education concerns habit formation. There are those to whom the assumption by the schools of any responsibility for student habits appears to lead inevitably to educational confusion. I do not share this view. On the contrary, it seems to me clear that the schools are bound to play an exceedingly important role in the formation of habits. The questions are: How frankly do the schools acknowledge the role? How seriously do they play the part? How successfully do they carry it out?

It is a highly important fact that the first sustained systematic application that most children experience is in the classroom. Work habits, with most children, are *made in school*. This is conspicuously the case, of course, in so far as the work habits have to do with intellectual effort. It is of the utmost importance, therefore, that the school face explicitly its responsibility for these work habits and take appropriate measures for assuring their satisfactory formation. In the early acquisition of sound habits of work lies a good share of subsequent individual growth and development.

What are the characteristics of the habits that need to be acquired? Doubtless the list might be made long. I mention only a few that seem most important: persistence, reliability, patience, courage, initiative, an accountability to one's own standards of excellence. Too commonly the school tolerates passable results, to the impairment of the habits of work. Students need to experience the satisfactions to be derived from tasks done to the best of their capacities. They need to

10

be taught the values of self-initiated and self-directed endeavor. In fact, self-driven education needs to become a firmly-established personal habit. Only when education becomes an individually-accepted responsibility are desirable outcomes assured. In this connection, general education faces some of its most essential obligations. Good work habits are hard to form; they dissolve rapidly in the acid of slovenly practices. General education must see that they are much more successfully nurtured by many classroom procedures than they are now.

In addition to the attention to be given to work habits, care must be exercised to promote better health habits. On the side of physical health much has been done and is being done; on the side of mental health, school procedures are still largely hit-or-miss. To a considerable extent well-grounded techniques directed toward mental hygiene are not yet in hand, but progress is being made, and ultimately the schools can do a great deal. That general education must accept serious responsibilities for the physical, mental, and emotional health of young people in the schools cannot be seriously questioned.

(3) A third group of responsibilities of general education has to do with the cultivation of interests, sensitivity, and appreciation. It is through the expansion and elevation of the range of spontaneous response that the prevailing culture is ultimately to be improved. Fortunately, there is in most young people a vast deal of native curiosity, a wide range of initial sensitiveness, a large reservoir of fresh appreciations. These potentialities the schools must realize and capitalize. Social sensitivity needs to be fostered, the love of beauty cultivated, intellectual drive stimulated, avocational and recreational hobbies induced. During childhood, inter-

11

ests are narrow and self-centered. Gradually the child's universe of acquaintance and interest must be expanded and objectified. Happily, the means by which we may all satisfy many of our desires are now so enlarged, and through public institutions and services—e.g., our parks, our libraries, our museums—made so widely and freely accessible, that the enrichment of life has become in substantial measure a matter of awakening and establishing worth-while, many-sided interests. Herein lie the possibilities of a durable zest in living. It is to be noted that our better schools are already demonstrating what can be done along this line. In the development of wider and more worthy interests, general education faces one of its clearest and most important opportunities.

(4) In the spread of knowledge and understanding general education carries still another set of responsibilities. In a sense, these are its traditional responsibilities. Through general education, students are expected to acquire knowledge of the physical universe, the social order, the cultural heritage. To a considerable extent, students do acquire such knowledge. They might acquire more than they do, however, even with no greater outlay of time and effort, if study materials were less extensively organized as formal, logical, systematic disciplines, unrelated to the backgrounds and interests of the learner. After all, if the goal be appreciative understanding of the world about us, the learning arrangements must be so set as to make possible a clear contact with the world *in which the learner lives.*

This principle becomes even more controlling as the school moves into certain new and relatively undeveloped fields in which the attainment of better understanding is of supreme importance. I refer to the fields of human development and human relations. To a surprising extent formal education

12

has failed to deal with some of the matters which concern us most intimately and affect us most vitally. What is the nature of human development in its physical, mental, emotional, and social phases? How are the normal and the pathological conditions to be distinguished? Of what do wholesome human relations consist, and what forms do they take? Questions such as these serve to suggest areas of human experience in which more understanding, widely diffused, is greatly to be desired. The responsibilities of general education in the promotion of understanding are well established and clear. What they need is substantial redirection and more effective implementation in concrete school programs.

(5) A supremely important group of responsibilities of general education relates to the inculcation of attitudes. Here again there are those who will resist the idea that general education should acknowledge any such purpose. As a matter of fact, the schools cannot possibly avoid a large measure of responsibility for attitudes. This follows partly from the fact that other agencies are unwilling or unable to assume the burden, and partly from the more important fact that for youth pervasive influences inhere in the very nature of school experiences. For good or bad, the schools are bound to affect the attitudes of those who attend them.

If in this connection we think of the schools as playing a primary part in the transmission and perpetuation of American culture, we are bound to ask what elements in this American culture call especially for the inculcation of attitudes. The answer lies in large measure in the concepts and traditions of American democracy. Democracy, at least in its American version, consolidates two basic doctrines: (1) the maximization of individual growth and development through freedom and the largest possible equalization of in-

13

dividual opportunities; and (2) the settlement of controversies between groups or classes of individuals by peaceful means, through resort to discussion, persuasion, the ballot, acceptance, and appraisal. On the one hand is an ideal of social progress; on the other, a way of social adjustment. On the one hand is an urge toward a broad and expanding humanitarianism; on the other, a commitment to the ways of peace in human association. If adherence to these popular ideals means some sacrifice of the immediate national efficiency, the American people are prepared to see this price paid; even at a cost, the fundamental doctrines of the American democracy are to be respected. It is within the framework of these doctrines that American history has been written. It is to these doctrines that the loyalties of the American people are pledged. It is in these doctrines that the core of American culture is to be found. With the transmission of these doctrines from generation to generation the American schools must be profoundly concerned.

What I have just stated is something more than a plea for a typical program of Americanization. What the schools need to get at is a constellation of attitudes. As a social order, we face growing collectivism. Of this, there cannot be the slightest doubt. No longer can the common interest be thought to emerge as the net resultant of the interplay of freely activated individual enterprises. No longer, in other words, can we rely so largely on the invisible hand of Providence, so often cited by the classical economists. The individualism we have known has played its part. On the whole, it has played it well. But it must give place now to a tempered, moderated individualism, effectively conditioned to serve the public interest.

One of the fundamental bases for such a new individual-

14

ism is to be found in the early shaping of individual attitudes in actual social situations. School life is a succession of social situations. For the young, these situations can be made real and vital. They can be made, through actual responsible participation, to inculcate appropriately socialized individual attitudes. Consideration for others, friendliness, sympathetic understanding of associates, toleration of individual differences of character and ability and opinion, fair play, team play, honesty, willing co-operation, wise leadership, loyalty to group interests, a desire for justice— these are among the attitudes that can be fostered. Obviously, the desired results are not to be obtained by mere platitudinous preachments; they require wise and adroit handling of a wide variety of educational procedures. If school activities consistently stress the competitive, at times the combative, one type of individual will emerge; if school activities commonly and constructively take co-operative forms, a different type of individual will appear. At bottom, the problem is one of balance: the values residing in individual achievement must be in substantial measure preserved, while the values to be secured from successful co-operation must be fostered. The possibilities along this line can only be realized as educators recast school procedures with wise regard to the attitudes to be induced. That the possibilities are of great significance seems to be self-evident. It is in this sector of the educational front that the schools may wisely "dare to build a new social order."

Let me add one further word about attitudes. Adherence to the American tradition of democracy should not be left by the schools to chance, nor to the ineffectual, and essentially misdirected, methods of instruction now commonly employed. The youth of the nation should be made familiar

15

with the heroic efforts through which individual freedom, after centuries of struggle, was finally achieved. They should be made to appreciate the incalculable values which individual freedom brings to human aspiration and achievement. They should be made to see that resort to force as a mode of social adjustment is a negation of the principles on which American ways of life are based. They should acquire an unswerving loyalty to the American tradition of democracy. They should be led to work for it, to devote themselves to it. In the inculcation of fundamental attitudes general education in America faces its gravest responsibilities.

The outcomes which have been cited can only become real and effective as they are embodied in the individual lives of oncoming youth. This involves the fundamental problem of achieving personal integration in growth and development. It is this integration in the individual, not integration in the curriculum, that is the fundamental consideration. Skills, habits, interests, understanding, and attitudes have to be cultivated and established as an organic whole, and with a nice regard to the capacity of the individual to submit to change and to effect a sustained personal development. An underlying sense of personal adequacy and security is indispensable. This is best attained through successful use of one's own expanding powers. As competence is demonstrated, self-assurance grows. As self-assurance develops, competence increases. Gradually there emerges a power to deal with significant new situations and experiences. Of course, the innate conditions of individual growth and the stubborn facts of the physical and social environment raise obstacles; these must be recognized in seeking the attainment of all educational objectives, but the maintenance of the integrated personality has always to be a governing principle.

16

Let me state the objectives of general education in another way:

1. We must make education connect more directly and explicitly with the forthright pursuit of truth. This is true of education at all levels and of all types. Too many students move through our schools and colleges without ever acquiring a firsthand acquaintance with what it means to seek truth honestly and faithfully. The experience is one which can be given within widely varying levels of intellectual capacity and educational endowment. The love of truth and the disinterested pursuit of it lie at the very heart of freedom. They should be cultivated assiduously through the work of our schools and colleges.

2. We must do better than we have in imparting through formal education a widespread social understanding. We have been too easily satisfied with evidences of information on the part of our students. Information is not enough. We must build information into knowledge, and knowledge into understanding. The common man must know where he is and where he is going; the character of the leadership he is offered and the requisites of the followership he must exhibit. Formal education must contribute more than it has to social wisdom.

3. We must make education minister more effectively than it has to an expanding social sympathy. Mankind is being knit more and more closely together. We must all come to see more clearly the nature and force of the common bonds of humankind the world over. The schools and colleges, especially as they learn to use some of the new devices, such as the teaching film, can make highly important contributions to this end.

4. We must through education give work an improved

17

status. There are few things in life so rewarding as a satisfactory job, and few things as unprofitable as sheer idleness. Leisure there should be when we have learned how to use it to advantage, but work itself should give its enduring satisfactions. The idea that we seek education in part to lighten our work load is basically fallacious. The more education we get, the greater are our obligations to serve. We must develop through popular education a philosophy of work in which productive labor becomes both a duty and a privilege. It is a responsibility of the schools and colleges to see that satisfaction is taken by students in work well done. It is equally important that young people get a clear conception of the rewards that lie in honest and sustained industry, be the occupation high or low.

5. Finally, we must in education in America come to grips with the everlasting moral imperatives of a free society. Our public schools and colleges have avoided this assignment all too long. Whatever may be necessary consequences of the complete separation of church and state, they surely do not entail avoidance of all moral responsibilities. Formal education cannot possibly be regarded as an amoral social function. It is high time that our schools and colleges dealt more explicitly and responsibly with their obligations to the moral order in American democracy.

Let it not be thought that the foregoing analysis of the responsibilities of general education in America is for the most part so general in its conclusions that no specific teaching content is indicated. On the contrary, the responsibilities that have been noted can be translated into concrete school procedures. It is of great importance that they be so translated, and so translated with imagination and social vision. Moreover, it is of great importance that measures be developed (as they can be) for ascertaining the extent to which the stated aims are attained and the responsibilities successfully discharged. It is time that general education in the United States was brought to more strict accountability. It is not too much to ask that larger results in social competence, in esthetic appreciation, in intellectual capacity, in common understanding and human sympathy should mark the graduates of our schools. The stakes are so great that no avoidable risks of failure can be permitted. Unless we are prepared to abandon our cherished American ways of life, the basic responsibilities of general education must be clearly identified and effectively met, and met with a minimum of delay.

Attempts to identify outcomes in concrete detail ordinarily result in a multiplicity of specific objectives. While all of these may be deserving, their very number serves to introduce a measure of diffusion, if not of confusion, in the direction of educational activities. What is needed is a system of priorities. Certain objectives must be recognized as primary in importance, others as secondary or tertiary. It is hardly necessary to add that these ideas of relative importance may reasonably reflect the particular needs of a given phase of political, economic, or social organization and development.

The potential impact of the *total educational enterprise* has to be considered in seeking the attainment of some of the objectives of *general* education. Extra-curricular as well as curricular activities have to be brought into consideration. Thus the operation of a student union, or the promotion of an effective organization for student self-government, may contribute significantly to the attainment of important skills and the establishment of indispensable attitudes and ideals.

19

It is only through a consistent *total* educational experience that we can hope to reach certain of the goals of *general* education.

This points to the necessity of integration. Efforts to sharpen the objectives of general education—or to make them more specific—must not be allowed to result in fragmentation of the educational program. Certain units of instruction may be required in order to pull things together. More essential, however, is an explicit educational philosophy governing the entire operation in all its parts.

Total education, as the biggest single force in the development and conservation of human resources, has surpassing importance. For a world in conflict it becomes absolutely essential that this great force be given as sharp and sure a direction as educational statesmanship can achieve. Hence reexamination, reappraisal and redirection of the educational enterprise are all from time to time in order. They surely are in order now. Basic planning activities have had too little attention. It is high time that educational institutions make such planning a matter of major concern.

Education for Democratic Ideals

Educational policy is essentially a segment of social policy, and no educational program stands a chance that is not wisely adapted to the social situation in which it has to be conducted. It would be foolish to undertake any full account of just where we stand as a people. However, as background for what I have to say about education for democracy, certain large components of our present predicament need to be recognized. These I propose just to mention:

First, we must recognize the widespread destruction wrought by the two world wars fought within a single generation. No one will ever calculate the total losses which these conflicts have entailed. We do know that the wastes in human death and injury, in direct property damage, and in social disruption will burden civilization for countless years to come.

We suffer, too, from the wholesale shattering of checks and balances upon which the smooth functioning of our economic system has depended. Contemporary economic activity is a vast mechanism of intricate equilibria which, thrown out of accustomed relationship to one another, develop distortions which are well-nigh unmanageable. Price and rate structures, government finances, flows of essential materials,

21

exchanges of goods and services in both domestic and foreign trade are concrete examples. It will take time and wise and courageous management to get these activities back in normal alignment once more. Meanwhile, the social costs of the current maladjustments are enormous.

We are paying huge penalties, too, for the shifts of economic and political power which invariably accompany the conduct of great wars. Certain important groups have come into strategic positions to which they are quite unaccustomed. As is almost invariably the case, they are abusing the powers of which they have suddenly come into possession. When organizations of labor, however commendable their aims, take the public by the throat and defy even the highest governmental authorities, the situation has come to an intolerable pass. Until corrective measures can be devised and applied, this type of affliction will impose appalling losses on our entire economy.

In America we have seen these arbitrary abuses of power largely in the conflict of economic groups. Over the world, however, some of the most serious conflicts are currently associated with vast popular uprisings. Great wars have a way of inducing great social upheavals. Momentous upsurgings of nationalistic and racialistic populations now characterize the international scene. They may prove to have momentous consequence for us.

Certainly not less formidable for the future of society is the latest phenomenal advance of physical science. The emergence of nuclear force has called a dramatic turn in human affairs. Without a shadow of doubt we have in the newly acquired command of atomic energy a power with which the whole world must reckon—a power for which the world seems as yet quite unprepared.

22

Finally, we must recognize that human affairs are currently confronted with a world-wide conflict of ideologies. The contending ideologies constitute a world force of immeasurable dimensions.

I have given this thumbnail sketch of the present state of the world for one reason alone—to bring out the fact that present conditions are not propitious for the way of life to which we in America aspire. Democratic ideals are hard to maintain at any time. They are especially difficult to maintain in a world that is economically and politically disordered and distraught. Yet that is the kind of world we now have. In all this uncertainty and confusion, the most ominous of the forces which condition our future are those relating to the conflict of ideologies. Our democracy is now under direct attack. The most fundamental question facing America today is this: Will the years ahead strengthen the cause of democracy or play into the hands of dictators?

Ours is a democratic tradition. We pride ourselves that we live in a land of the free. We cherish our great civil liberties. We rejoice in our strength as a great self-governing people. But in the kind of world we have today, there is no assurance that this priceless heritage will remain ours unless we make supreme efforts to protect it. Unless we train specifically for democracy, we are liable to lose it.

Training for democracy presupposes a clear conception of what democracy is. We have heard a lot of talk about the nature of our democratic ways of life. Some of what has been written on the subject is to the point; much of it is vague and not designed to afford any adequate basis for a working program. The best brief statement I have seen on the subject came from the pen of the distinguished historian, the late Carl Becker. I quote:

To have faith in the dignity and worth of the individual man as an end in himself, to believe that it is better to be governed by persuasion than by coercion, to believe that fraternal good will is more worthy than a selfish and contentious spirit, to believe that in the long run all values are inseparable from the love of truth and the disinterested search for it, to believe that knowledge and the power it confers should be used to promote the welfare and happiness of all men rather than to serve the interests of those individuals and classes whom fortune and intelligence endow with temporary advantage—these are the values which are affirmed by the traditional democratic ideology. They are the values which, since the time of Buddha and Confucius, Solomon and Zoroaster, Plato and Aristotle, Socrates and Jesus, men have commonly employed to measure the advance or the decline of civilization, the values they have celebrated in the saints and sages.*

If we accept this compact statement of democratic ideals, how are we to move into concrete programs designed to train for their attainment? We naturally think first of formal education, of the work of the schools and colleges.

Here the picture is by no means clear. Generally speaking, it may be said that the schools and colleges of this country do a better job of democratic education than is done in any other country of the world. The fact remains, however, that they leave much to be desired.

For example, the standard required courses in American history certainly yield wholly inadequate results. In saying this I am not referring to the ignorance of our students of dates, names, and places. I refer rather to their failure through these courses to capture the fundamental elements

* *New Liberties for Old* (New Haven: Yale University Press, 1942), p. 149 f.

of American life. What we need to do is to bring our youth through formal education to a real appreciation of the central core of our democratic tradition, to an understanding of the nature of the contributions of the men and women who have made America great, to an unswerving loyalty to the specific ways and means by which we have kept this land a land of opportunity and liberty.

Similarly, in other phases of the social studies in the schools we must strive to achieve fundamental social understanding and genuine economic literacy at all levels of American society. For example, we must induce universal recognition of the fact that what we do not produce, we cannot consume, that only as we increase the real wealth of the country can we expect steadily to raise our already high standard of living. We must have a doctrine of productivity in American life. Our youth must be brought to see that industry, thrift and self-reliance are still cardinal virtues. They must learn, too, that there are limits on the extent to which we can wisely entrust our lives to the state.

Moreover, in our formal education at all levels we must abandon, once and for all, the idea that it is not the task of our schools and colleges to deal with moral and spiritual values. We cannot go on tolerating the failure of the schools to deal constructively with the inculcation of habits and ideals of simple honesty. In both curricular and extra-curricular activities, the enduring values of honorable living must be cultivated by all available means. Performance without character and ambition without integrity threaten to be our undoing.

The challenge to formal education which lies in the general area of training for democracy is so sweeping that its importance cannot possibly be exaggerated. Nothing short of a universal discipline of mind and heart and body will serve to pull us through the crisis in which we now find ourselves. There are no short cuts to virtue. The ideals of conduct upon which our liberty ultimately depends can be instilled only by a comprehensive and concerted effort on a national scale. This is no mere wishful thinking; it is inescapable practical politics.

Needless to say, no vast undertaking of this sort will be successfully accomplished by formal education alone. Like influence must be brought to bear through church and home. More and more it becomes clear that there is no lasting substitute for the contributions which have been traditionally made by these indispensable social institutions. Much of the molding of youth of which we are so greatly in need can still best be effected by parents. We have forgotten this fact altogether too frequently in American life in recent years. To do what is required, parents must be ready to devote time, thought, and patience. Any delegation of this responsibility invites results which parents themselves deplore. Only as home, church, and school, as well as other character-building agencies, collaborate in training for democracy are we likely to preserve our democratic way of life.

It certainly would be giving an inadequate account of the requirements of this great undertaking if mention were not made of the mass media which now play so constantly on the mind and heart of people of all ages and of every class. In many ways some of the forces currently exerted by these mass media make the work of home, church, and school much more difficult than it would otherwise be. If the press, the pulp magazines, the comic strips, the motion picture, television, and the radio are put together, one is bound to acknowledge an impact on the thinking, feeling, and aspiring of our people which at times threatens to negative all the efforts of the educators to promote a free and tolerant community. It is in this area that some of the most troublesome problems of training for democracy lie.

What should we be doing to strengthen the hold which democratic ideals have upon us? I will venture to give the answer very briefly for formal education. The answer here falls into four parts:

First, we must come to see the issues more clearly. We must set certain definite ideals, separating the more important from the less important. As we plan concrete programs and introduce educational innovations, we must keep constantly in mind some such analysis of the essentials of democracy as I cited from Becker. It is these essentials which must be translated into a concrete educational program, using revised curricula, modern teaching aids, such as the film and education broadcast, and all sorts of extra-curricular activities, in short, all of the operations of the school.

In the second place, we must take education more seriously than we have. The American people exhibit interest in education to an extraordinary extent. No subject is more widely discussed. Many people think they know something about it. But rarely is education viewed seriously enough even to discover that it is a complex and intricate art which can easily miscarry. In the long run we can get from it what we demand, but we can get this only as we come to think of it as in many ways man's most important single undertaking.

In the third place, we must support education even more generously than we have. School teachers are paid today at a level which is incredibly low, in fact, so low that teachers by the thousands are now abandoning teaching as a career.

27

If we are to get the service in education of which we are so clearly in need, we must be prepared to pay for it. This means that we must be prepared to give compensation which will draw into the teaching profession men and women capable of rendering the kind of high service we must have if we are to train successfully for democracy. Educational budgets may be high in this country, but if we are well advised, we shall make them higher. Only through more generous support can we get the results of which I have been speaking.

Finally, of even greater importance than any rate of compensation for teaching is an improved status for the teacher. In terms of the social hierarchy of American life, the teacher has a position which is commensurate with the teacher's low pay. Only when we come to think of teachers as among the most valuable of public servants, are we likely to attract into the teaching profession men and women of the capacity and fortitude required in the invaluable service we expect of them.

In short, we shall get the kind of formal education requisite to adequate training for democracy if and when we demand it and are prepared to foot the bill. This is a large "if," and an "if" of tremendous consequence. For the world of tomorrow belongs to ideas and ideals, not to material forces. Not that material forces will not assume proportions never before witnessed, but the use to which these great forces will be put will be ultimately determined by the ideas and ideals of the people. What we must achieve, therefore, is essentially an intellectual, moral, and spiritual reformation.

In short, the time is now upon us when we must change our ways to meet the requirements of a new world—a world which within our own generation has been twice seized by great convulsions and now is at a critical parting of the ways.

28

If the bomb that dropped on Hiroshima on August 6, 1945, proved anything, it was that the physical powers now in man's possession are quite as capable of destroying civilization as they are of building it. It follows that in the mind and heart of mankind, and not in any array of physical forces, our whole future lies. It is only as the mind and heart of mankind prove equal to the task now before us that we and our successors can possibly hope to prosper. And if we are to remain free, there is no more important enterprise than that of effectively training for democratic ideals. Why should we not recognize it as such and devote to it all the resources we can possibly bring to bear, at home and abroad, in public and in private, and assuredly here and now?

Changes in the Organization of

American Public Education

As WE scan the future of education in the United States, we certainly cannot foresee all the changes that will take place, but I believe that we can see at least some of the "handwriting on the wall." It behooves us to know what these visible signs are, so that we may participate in the wise planning of the movements which presumably lie ahead. Doubtless we shall go through a period during which relatively little attention will be given to some of the far-reaching changes in the educational structure that seem destined to come as soon as we can get back to our peacetime pursuits. I am, therefore, discussing the modifications that lie beyond the war emergency, in the period of the next generation or two, as we adjust our educational organization to what appear to be profound changes in the social order and economic system which have already come upon us and rather clearly call for serious modifications in our educational undertakings. Before I undertake to outline what these changes of educational structure are likely to be if we handle the matter wisely, let me indicate a few of the developments which are bound to determine their course.

1. *Economic changes.* The most obvious and most im-

portant of these is the situation in which youth finds itself as a result of the great transformations of modern industry, particularly with respect to early employment. Of course, it may be that the frightful unemployment of the 1930's was but a passing phase in the maturation of our economic system. Frankly, I doubt whether that is so. I am inclined to think, on the contrary, that the opportunities for full-time employment for young people are going to remain more or less permanently restricted. It seems to me that we have to plan in terms of relatively limited private opportunities for full-time work for young people up to the age of at least twenty or twenty-one years. We have already witnessed the consequences of this economic situation as it has been reflected in the plight of youth over a period of several years. One of the most appalling aspects of the depression of the 1930's was the idleness of our young people. Millions of these youngsters were out of work, chronically, over a period of years. That, in my opinion, is a maladjustment which no social order can wisely tolerate. It packs too much political dynamite. The surprising thing is that we rode through that situation in the 1930's with as little disturbance as we had. Idle youth is material for all sorts of revolutionary developments. What we witness in Europe had its origin in part in youthful frustration. No society that leaves its youth in idleness can long endure.

This is the most important factor to have in mind in calculating the reorganization of public education: reorganization must make provision for extending the formal education of youth from the ages of sixteen or seventeen to twenty or twenty-one. Thus far in this country we have not faced up to this situation. We hear a good deal of complaint about the demoralization of secondary education. I think

31

much of that criticism is not only unfair but also ignorant. It is laid against the schools with no recognition of the task faced by the schools of today, nor of the efforts that have been made to meet it. The fact remains that the task of the schools has become enormously more difficult and complicated than it was, and that there is little evidence that the schools have yet met the new requirements adequately.

2. *Vocational education.* A second observation that I would make in terms of the type of educational reorganization which lies in prospect has to do with the motivation on which we must depend in working out the new program. I am familiar with the contempt that exists in some educational quarters for education that is vocationally motivated. Vocational education is supposed to be education of an inferior sort, something to be avoided, a sort of academic prostitution. Apparently these critics think that any interest in a future job is something impure, something that should be refined out of education. I do not share such views. I think there is something essentially sound and wholesome about vocational interests. The most natural, the most inescapable interest of young people is in a job. A job is the means of satisfying the other worth-while demands of youth. Young people want to establish homes, to have children, to develop a lot of other worth-while interests. The full-time, compensated job is the means of achieving these aims. I see nothing improper or unworthy in the absorption that young people evidence in a satisfactory working career. No free society in which an interest and a devotion to work do not constitute prime moving urges has a real future.

On a statue at Tuskegee Institute there is carved this excerpt from a speech given by Booker T. Washington: "We shall prosper in proportion as we learn to dignify and glorify labor." We shall prosper in America, as a free people, as we learn to dignify and glorify labor. I think that it is tragic beyond words to tolerate an economic system which does not provide satisfactory work opportunities for all; and it is certainly tragic when youth, seeking employment, finds none. We must think in terms of a school for our total youth population which runs further than the grades ordinarily provided even in our present secondary-school program. We must extend common, universal education beyond grade twelve to provide educational opportunities for young people up to the age of twenty-one. We must articulate the education provided with suitable training and placement in the starting of careers which are going to prove satisfying to our young people.

3. *Education for Democracy*. In the third place we must never be satisfied with education which is purely vocational, which has no purpose but to get youth on to its first job. We must develop a continuing and pervasive interest on the part of all youth in the meaning and importance of democracy. It is essential that we give youth a live, alert, and enduring interest in our free society; that we help them to know what it means; how it is threatened; how it may be strengthened over the years; what price would be entailed if it were lost or seriously impaired; what the world struggle is about, and where they as young freemen must take their stand in that struggle. This interest transcends all individual interests, and can give invaluable satisfactions as it works itself out in the kind of devotion which every individual in a free society must feel.

Of course, we must introduce also cultural and esthetic elements to insure an education which is fully commendable. However, these other essentials of which I have spoken are

33

the elements without which we cannot maintain the society in which our culture must be nourished. And so, I believe:

That we face an entirely new problem with reference to the extension of free, universal education. It must carry our youth population further than it has in the past; presumably not only up through grade twelve, but probably on up through grade fourteen, so as to train and guide young people up to the time when they can be inducted into full-time employment. If local public education comes to be extended through an additional two grades, including what is now the lower division of college education, profoundly important changes in the whole structure of American higher education may occur in the course of time. As matters now stand, professional education is pressing in from the top and junior college education pressing in from underneath. It is not at all unlikely that ultimately we shall have in the basic system of public education in this country a 6-4-4 arrangement; in other words, a six-year elementary school, a four-year high school, and a four-year collegiate institution at the top.

That education, in its upper reaches, must be substantially vocational in purpose and in content. It must give young people capacities for the job; not narrow specialties, but capacities for broad opportunities according to their interests, their drives, and their abilities, and, of course, with reference to opportunities for remunerative work.

That we must always have in mind the social necessity of so conducting education that we shall get, as an end result, an understanding, alert, appreciative devotion, as well as an unflinching loyalty, to our free institutions and our democratic way of life.

What does this mean with relation to how all this can

34

be organized? We are committed to the common elementary school, deep-rooted in our American society and no longer challenged by anyone. The battle over that has been won. I think, upon the whole, we can say that we have also won the battle for some kind of universal education through the secondary school. On top of the elementary school, we may now wisely think of another common school, of secondary character, in which all children should be found, of whatever complexion or capacity; one in which great emphasis should be placed upon diagnosis of what the young people are and what they are likely to become, of their qualities of mind and spirit, of their individual differences. Inside that second common school, the process of differentiation should set in. The process of formal classification on the basis of a careful, fully developed diagnosis should begin at this level.

On top of this second common school, I think we shall have to develop, in the course of time, a battery of differentiated institutions or schools of a more specialized nature which will accommodate all the young people, girls as well as boys. There are many differences among them, of course. There are some who lean naturally in the direction of the intellectual life; many others do not. Some students will look toward the fine arts; some, toward the practical. There are great differences amongst these youngsters: they do not all respond alike to education; they have different sets of motivating principles; their learning processes vary widely. We shall need to divide our educational patterns in terms of drives and abilities at this level. By the time the youngsters reach grades nine and ten, and certainly as they go on to grades eleven to fourteen, we shall need to provide radically different programs of instruction. It is possible that for many we shall have to combine education with industrial, agricultural, or other vocational experiences, under some co-operative plan worked out between educators and employers. We certainly cannot successfully service the total youth population by passing out the same kind of fare to all, or by trying to maintain uniformly the traditions of the academic high school. That just will not do. It is because we have tried to do this that so many youngsters are out of school now instead of in school. Going to school is the last thing many of them now want to do; they have passed the limit of desire for formal education of the kind that has been offered. Learning should be essentially an interesting, if not a fascinating, experience. Learning only becomes unpleasant as a result of attempted forcing when it is not served in the right form or in the proper setting. We shall have to go definitely vocational in the setting for many of our youngsters. We shall have to say, "This is the way in which you will be moved effectively and successfully into your first job." I believe that education of this type will need to be supplied largely, or wholly, within the public school system.

A recent inquiry by-passes the problem of the junior college. It says in substance, "Let some of the high schools develop two additional years." Apparently the inquiry thought this not a major problem. I do not think that made real sense; I believe that the problem is one of the most pressing in American education. What are we going to do at this level? We cannot say to youth, "We haven't the school that fits your interests and needs. Hang around and look for a job." Out-of-school youth is too much of a threat! This is a serious social problem, and it must be solved in terms of educational development.

The state will need to sit down with this whole problem

and solve it. If the state solves it, it is going to mean that the youth of the state will, in one way or another, be provided with effective education through grade fourteen, largely at public expense.

The problem here is vital also to our institutions of higher learning. Sooner or later the state must face the serious situation which exists in the colleges. What will happen to those institutions when local units take on the job of servicing youth through the first two years of college? Liberal arts colleges, agricultural colleges, and others must give fairly elaborate offerings looking toward the major occupations available to persons prepared at the higher levels. I do not believe that the more educational prerequisites we put into a given kind of training, the better it will go. We may have gone too far in extending professional training in certain fields, and I question whether we can continue in this direction indefinitely. An unduly protracted period of formal education will not be indefinitely tolerated; it invites the criticism that it introduces preference for those who are privately endowed. We may have already gone too far in extending formal education preparatory to certain great professions. In other cases, I think we can wisely extend present programs. I approve, for example, the recent move of New York State in requiring prospective secondary-school teachers to take a fifth year at the college level. There are at least three or four professions which ought to think in terms of formal training to just about that extent; business administration is one. If the process at the lower levels is worked out satisfactorily, and if, too, we service well our young people and keep our society free, there will have to be numerous adjustments at the college level.

What about the costs of this whole undertaking? They

will be substantially higher than the costs of present high-school education. It will all be expensive if it is well adjusted to vocational training.

In New York State there will have to be a large amount of assistance. New York State does not begin to put as much into public higher education as do the other states. Sooner or later it will have to catch up. I start with the premise that New York State is powerful and that it has great resources; that it is going to provide as good educational facilities as other states and on terms which are just as favorable as those of any other state. These surely are sound premises. If so, New York State must give more financial aid in the upper reaches of education. That does not necessarily mean tax-supported institutions, but it does mean tax-supported educational opportunities.

Let me mention some of the principal difficulties lying in the way of this program of educational reorganization:

1. *The difficulty of financing the program.* It will be financed adequately only as the people are fully persuaded that it is a necessary program, that it must be done even at a sacrifice. A lot of educating of the people will be necessary before this is accomplished, because many feel that the expense is already excessive. There will doubtless be resistance to this program, for if it goes through, more public funds will need to be spent.

Some of the most obvious and most discussed issues confronting higher and professional education relate to financial support. The current difficulties and unfavorable prospects of the private institutions in this respect are a matter of common knowledge. Declining interest rates over the past years have dropped the yield on endowment funds. By shifting somewhat the composition of investment portfolios and by improving noticeably the investment practices, the finance committees of certain institutions have apparently succeeded in temporarily arresting this downward trend of endowment yields. The chances are, however, that this is only a temporary success. A further decline in the rate of interest is probable. Meanwhile it becomes increasingly difficult for the private institutions to raise additional endowment funds. Large private fortunes are not being accumulated as frequently as in the past, are subject to much heavier taxation, and are likely to be more tightly held. Adding to the financial worries of the private institutions is the possibility—one may safely say, probability—that the number of students seeking the type of education they have to offer on the terms at which they offer it will diminish in the course of time so considerably as to cut seriously into tuition receipts. The financial outlook of the private institutions is, in short, one that may reasonably occasion widespread anxiety.

It has been commonly thought that the public institutions are happily immune from any such worries. It has to be admitted, of course, that by and large the tax-supported colleges and universities have enjoyed during recent years a financial stability denied to the private institutions, but there is reason to believe that the public institutions now face their own set of increasing financial difficulties. These will stem in general from tremendous increases in the demands made upon the public treasury. At the moment defense requirements are given the right of way and are involving huge expenditures. A public debt of astronomical dimensions appears to be inevitably ahead and will doubtless impose on available tax receipts an exceedingly heavy burden of debt service. Social security and such relief programs as may seem necessary to take care of the unemployed have doubtless come to stay and are sure to involve an increasing financial load. Social reforms, such as slum clearance and health protection, are almost certain to receive increased attention, and will doubtless impose additional burdens upon the public treasury. More ample educational facilities at the secondary-school and junior-college levels will compete with the higher institutions for public support. Even a cursory consideration of all these impending developments leads to the conclusion that public, as well as private, institutions for higher and professional education face times that will be financially difficult.

2. *Persuading a free society to adopt the processes of selective education.* We have oversold education in this country to such an extent that all people, parents and young people alike, entertain the idea that the more education, the better. They think of the number of years of education, not of the outcomes for the learner. They say with pride, "My boy went through college." That idea has been completely "sold" to the American people, and the result is that attitudes toward higher education are undiscriminating. How can we prevail on the young people who have been "diagnosed" in their earlier years in the common secondary school, and subsequently, to act intelligently on the basis of the diagnoses? For example, how can we succeed in getting a lad to attend a mechanics' institute and abandon the hope of becoming a great lawyer?

That, I think, is a most difficult problem. We shall face the same kind of question if we try to extend state aid, in the form of scholarships, in the higher reaches of education. Suppose, for example, that in New York State we should award one hundred and fifty full-cost state scholarships to young men and women wishing to become doctors. Undoubtedly several thousand persons would compete for them. How could we satisfy those who did not receive financial assistance that the system was fair? If state authorities were in a position to award such scholarships on any system they cared to set up, there would be grief. We should, for example, probably have to use a purely scholastic test of aptitude for medical training, and that would be a step backward. The task of developing ways and means of discriminating wisely and fairly among our young people in connection with the extension of larger educational opportunities at public expense is, in my opinion, one of the most difficult problems now confronting American public education.

The issues which relate to selective admission and promotion are important. Moreover, they are likely to come rapidly to the fore as more and more young persons successfully pass through the secondary school and seek higher education, and as opportunities for education at all levels are made more and more freely available. The theory until now has been that young people should be encouraged to go on with formal education just as long as they can meet the scholastic requirements and cover the necessary financial outlays. Economic considerations have been the determining factor in a host of cases. Selection on this basis has left much to be desired from the point of view of the most effective utilization of available human resources.

The Pennsylvania Study of the Carnegie Foundation brought out clearly the fact that, of the better half of high-school graduates, only about one-half go on to college, and, of the students who do go to college, about one-quarter are less qualified for higher education than one-half of the high-school graduates who do not succeed in going on to college. In other words, much of the student material the colleges get is inferior; and much of the student material that is superior the colleges do not get.

The same sort of distortion in the process of selection and promotion exists at other levels. There is, moreover, all-too-frequent dilution of student bodies through failure to select as rigorously as is necessary to maintain the standards which should characterize higher and professional education. Still another complication arises when the available facilities will not accommodate all those who are scholastically qualified to enter, as, for example, in medicine today. All of these situations, as well as others which might readily be cited, such as a possible extension of the system of state scholarships, point to the pressing need of improved methods of selective admission and promotion. What we must have is both an improved technical procedure and an improved administrative organization for the selective handling of students at all levels. The improved organization must include both private agencies and governmental offices operating in the field of education. Increasingly governmental authorities will be called upon to pick those who are to have specified educational privileges. It is of the utmost importance that this work of the public educational authorities be conducted with the highest attainable competence and with complete detachment from personal or partisan influences.

3. *Other problems lie in the limitations of professional vision among the educators of the country.* We still have much to do to expand the capacity to achieve a measure of intelligence, understanding, devotion, industry, and drive in the teachers and administrators commensurate with the job to be done. All teachers ought to understand what the problems are, what the available procedures and techniques are, and how the subject-matter specialties are to be knit to-

42

gether, so that they will service the young people and protect the interests of the democratic society into which they are moving. The teachers of the future must have a technical competence and an interest in this great profession exceeding anything we have ever seen.

Therein lies the great opportunity for a university school of education or for a department of education in a college. It is not a matter of thrusting trade education on a number of defenseless boys and girls. Education is mysterious business, and the learning process, a baffling one. There have to be infinite patience and deep understanding of what is involved, both psychologically and socially. There has to be a knowledge of the nature of the social problems and of the needs that must be served. It is a demanding kind of task that we face in education, but I, for one, cannot see anything that seems to me quite as important. If we are going to save this democracy of ours, it will be saved by the sort of educative process which, in its most intensive form, is represented by the work of the teacher. There must be much other education, but the bedrock of the whole process lies in the schools, or in the collaboration of the schools with the homes and the churches; and the teacher is one key necessary to the solution.

Educational Objectives and

Teacher Education

WHATEVER external calm we may succeed in maintaining these days, there lies underneath in each of us a deep and disturbing anxiety. The ideals and aspirations we have treasured, the peace we have cherished, the very essentials of our established way of life—all these and more are in jeopardy. If we are not to go totalitarian and seek the solution of our national problems through force, we have no alternative but to look to education for dealing effectively with the momentous issues with which we are now confronted. Basically our national defense is not primarily a matter of military, naval, and aeronautical forces; the great fortifications with which we must be particularly concerned are comprehended in the concept of our national morale. In this quarter, if authoritarian systems of compulsion are to be avoided, education—formal and informal—must be depended upon to provide necessary defenses. In the long run, the best safeguards against totalitarianism lie in a consolidated, adequately stabilized, progressive, free society. Educational undertakings of a comprehensive sort are indispensable in the creation of such a social order. The prompt improvement of public education in this country, and therewith the prompt improvement of teacher-education, must be regarded as an essential component of any program of comprehensive national defense.

Teacher-education is to be improved either through an improvement of the methods now employed in producing teachers, the goals of such education remaining substantially as they are, or through an extension and elevation of the objectives of such education, these changes of purpose resulting in the desired improvement of the outcomes. I propose to direct attention to those advances in teacher-education which can be achieved only through greater clarification and fundamental reorganization of the expressed purposes of education. After all, the improvement of teacher-education is a corollary of the improvement of education. Something needs to be said about what the improved teachers will be expected to accomplish after *their* improved education has become effective. Inquiry along this line leads us back to the functions of education in a democracy and the extent to which these functions are being recognized in current educational procedures.

In contemporary American society, the functions of education are pluralistic, not monistic; they are manifold and varied, not unitary. For example, we educate for one type of specific purpose in a medical internship or in a course in advanced mechanics in the upper division of a college of arts and sciences, but with a very different type of educational intent when we conduct a nursery school or provide a course in American history in a public high school. So, up and down the educational scale we recognize readily a wide variety of educational objectives. A good deal of the argument and confusion which has occurred in the discussion of education and

45

of teacher-training has arisen from a failure to identify these variant purposes of education.

The purposes of education being divergent, different instructional techniques and different sorts of teaching personnel are in order. Our present interest is largely in general public education at the elementary- and secondary-school levels. This concentration of interest does not imply that there is no need for improvement in the education of a college teacher—far from it. We have done too little about the professional education of the college teacher. The day is coming when we shall do much more about these teachers; but that is another story, and in any sustained effort along that line it must be frankly recognized that there are peculiar obstacles which do not exist, at any rate in anything like the same dimensions, at the lower levels of general education. While college education still resists rather stoutly any attempt at appraisal of classroom instruction, elementary- and secondary-school education has long since accustomed itself to a large amount of critical self-examination. This greatly facilitates the process of continuous improvement of general education at these levels.

American schools are expected to contribute to the preservation of the democratic system. This responsibility they share with other social agencies which contribute to general education in diverse and important ways. Some of the agencies which in times past have carried the larger share of the burden of general education have, during more recent times, been shedding considerable parts of this responsibility. This certainly has been true of the family and the church. Those responsibilities for the education of youth which are no longer being carried by the family and the church have been taken over by the school in considerable measure, though in part they have not yet been expressly lodged anywhere. By and large it is safe to say that the social agency which has the best chance of discharging successfully the great responsibility of transmitting the culture is the educational system maintained through public support. Certainly at the present time it is axiomatic that the American school has a grave responsibility in the continuous transmission of American democracy as a form of progressive, free society.

This profoundly important responsibility of public education in this country, if it is clearly recognized and effectively implemented, would seem to call for a serious reorganization of American education in a variety of directions. What is needed is a frank acknowledgment of the responsibility, not in vague generalities, but in concrete details, carefully to reconsider school programs. I am convinced that the public schools of this country have not earnestly and intelligently considered the nature of their responsibility in the transmission of our culture in its basic social, political, and moral ingredients. This failure is due in part to the fact that it has not been anyone's job to think of educational responsibilities in just these terms. Education in this country has been organized largely in terms of traditional disciplines of the mind. Thus the schools have taught the mother tongue and certain other languages. They have taught number systems from the simplest arithmetic to advanced mathematics. They have taught elements of science and technology. They have introduced a few units of instruction of history and the social studies. Put together, all these elements have produced an essentially segmented whole, rather well done in its individual parts but not producing in combination the essential total effect.

47

The important point is that we need to see more clearly than we have that no aggregate of individual subject-matter disciplines can be expected to give any assurance that certain essentials of the existing culture in America will be effectively transmitted from generation to generation. The schools may give young people a thorough mastery of the mother tongue, of the basic number system, of the elements of science and technology, and even a measure of social understanding, without providing young people with any clear insight into what is meant by progressive democracy, or a forward-moving, free society. Certainly there is nothing about an aggregate of subject-matter disciplines that will guarantee any enduring loyalties to the society in which the schools are carrying on their educational programs. Unhappily, as matters now stand, hundreds of thousands of our young people come to think of democracy as little more than that formal government under which all are privileged to do what they like. Certainly hosts of our young people are not today coming to realize that free society can be maintained only as the free citizens render a common service in a common cause. Specialties of the sort which are commonly taught in the schools, valuable as they may be in carrying on the culture, are not the most important elements of the culture. If we are to improve general education and the education of teachers, we must concern ourselves more intelligently and earnestly with the major functions of the schools in transmitting progressively the essential attributes of the free society in which we are all now privileged to live. That is the fundamental assignment for education and for teachers in America.

If it is agreed that this is the nature of the fundamental responsibility of the schools, large questions of reorientation and reorganization become inescapable. Without losing sight of some of the problems with which we have been concerned, we must entertain others. While we continue our efforts to improve instruction in the three R's, or in the so-called essentials, we must devote much more of our education to the ways and means of securing certain other outcomes in our school programs which we have discussed.

We hear much discussion of the professionalization of the public-school teacher. If by "professionalizing a teacher" is meant giving a teacher a misdirected training in *how* to teach, with no command of *what* to teach, then, of course, professionalizing stands self-condemned. If, however, what is meant is giving the teacher an adequate understanding of what teaching is about and what it is designed to accomplish, a thorough understanding of the process of learning as well as of teaching, and a thorough knowledge of the nature of the human material which underlies this process of learning; if what is meant is giving the teacher an adequate understanding of the nature of the devotion to public interest which goes with this great vocation—then the more we professionalize, the better. In one way or another, we shall have to break through the complacency which exists in a good many quarters with regard to the adequacy of training for teaching when it has failed to effect anything more than a technical equipment in an area of specialization.

In short, I think that we stand at a place in the broad highway on which education has traveled where we must decide which of two roads we are going to take. I do not believe that it is necessary to think of these roads in terms of any contrast between the essentialists and the progressives. The essentialists have been serving an excellent purpose. In so far as they have failed to recognize some of the larger respon-

49

sibilities of education, which the progressives have been emphasizing, they have been "offside." We can profession-alize partly in terms of an improved performance within specified limitations, some of which relate to the specific disciplines. Thus, we can improve the teaching of English, mathematics, history, and music. At the same time we need to assume added responsibilities which, up to this time, we have largely neglected. These responsibilities relate to the establishment of ideas, attitudes, understandings, loyalties, all of which are of the very essence of the living of free men in a free society. We must find ways and means of holding this system of ours despite the strains and stresses now placed upon it. We can do this by a constructive, farseeing program of innovation in the American schools.

HIGHER EDUCATION

A University and Its Functions

In some ways it is strange that it should be necessary to re-
affirm that the primary function of a university is to promote
the intellectual life. Yet so potent are the divisive and dis-
tracting forces of contemporary society that universities appear at times to be anything but centers of intellectual activity. Like other social institutions, they get caught in political
agitations, reform movements, recreational programs, and
social and community activities, with the inevitable result
that the intellectual drive loses primacy.

A great university should be a place in which there are
relatively undisturbed opportunities to live with ideas. Much
of life is otherwise engaged. But on campuses thoughtful men
and women, of faculty and student body alike, should be led
to seek out all sorts of ideas: ideas that are deeply rooted in
human experience; ideas that, like constellations in the intellectual firmament, have guided the earlier mariners of
human thought; ideas that have more recently opened the
doors of new knowledge of nature and of man; ideas that
afford the foundation of our systems of law and order, of
justice and liberty. Men and women on a campus should
learn how knowledge is gained and wisdom won. They
should, through practice, improve their command of the

53

difficult art of critical thinking. They should come to know something of the nature of imaginative and creative thinking. They should acquaint themselves with the heritage of accumulated wisdom. They should strive for intelligence. They should learn what it means to abide with reason. They should, through sustained effort, achieve accessions of intellectual power. They should, in brief, through their common interests and activities in the university, come to know what is meant by the intellectual life.

This is no academic plea. Nor is it an ideal that need not be too seriously taken. The place of intelligence in culture is being challenged in ways that may well give us pause. When men in power conclude that ideas should come from authority and not from thought, men of reason must give battle. The liberal tradition to which the democratic peoples owe allegiance cannot survive in a climate unfavorable to free inquiry. If the liberal tradition is to be sustained, there must be an unswerving belief in the capacity of the people for intelligent action; there must be a readiness on the part of the people to follow intelligent leadership; and there must be, wisely protected and adequately supported, centers of higher learning in which intelligence is assiduously cultivated and has free play.

This does not mean that our universities should become cloistered institutions, remote from the affairs of the day. They should accept exposure to the whole world of ideas and phenomena, including those of contemporary society. The intellectual life is not a life of quiet ease. Emerson spoke to this point when he said:

God offers to every mind its choice between truth and repose. Take which you please—you can never have both. Between these,

54

as a pendulum, man oscillates. He in whom the love of repose dominates will accept the first creed, the first philosophy, the first political party he meets—most likely his father's. He gets rest, commodity, and reputation; but he shuts the door to truth. He in whom the love of truth predominates will keep himself aloof from all moorings, and afloat. He will abstain from dogmatism, and recognize all the opposite negations, between which, as walls, his being is swung. He submits to the inconvenience of suspense and imperfect opinion, but he is a candidate for truth, as the other is not, and respects the highest law of his being.

"Candidates for truth"—that is what university men and women should be. Why are they not more uniformly so?

Two sets of forces operate to make it difficult for our universities to maintain the primacy of the intellectual function. The forces of the first set are external: they inhere in the nature of the surrounding culture.

Reference has been made to the eclipse of the liberal tradition. Force is in the field, armed, aggressive and arrogant. War in some quarters has become so natural a phase of governmental action that it no longer has to be declared. The outlook for peace-loving peoples is ominous. The life of the university is inevitably affected by this world situation.

Another external force of great potency is the love of money. To a dangerous degree we have come to regard the accumulation of wealth as the hallmark of individual success. Perhaps this was an unavoidable consequence of the stress laid, in conquering our continent, on ideals of free individual enterprise. But the love of money has dominated our social psychology to such an extent as to make the intellectual life appear pale and academic. The basic work of the universities becomes increasingly difficult as the intellectual life loses social esteem.

55

Closely affiliated with the love of money, though by no means identical with it, is the widely prevalent insistence upon vocational results in American education. Not that vocational aims are not to be granted a place in the organization of formal education. As a matter of fact, vocational interests constitute an invaluable aid over a wide range of educational undertakings. At times, and with certain types of students, education apparently cannot be made effective except as it is made primarily vocational. The essential difficulties arise from the fact that vocational interests are in many instances narrow in outlook and distressingly shortsighted as to the ways and means by which a durable vocational competence is to be developed. The best training for a position may be an enhancement of intelligence and intellectual power without explicit reference to the more technical skills the position requires. It is quite likely that most of these technical skills should be taught on the job, not in the school or college. In so far as the cultivation of the intellectual life in our universities is put under narrow vocational pressures, the primary purposes of the university are in some measure defeated.

The same type of consideration arises in connection with all sorts of practical demands upon our institutions of higher learning. Let me not be misunderstood. It is the duty of a great university to serve the society in which it carries on. But it is equally the duty of the university to apply its resources so as to maintain that service permanently. It is for the long pull that our universities exist. Practical men commonly want quick results. As a people we are afflicted at times with attacks of unwarranted impatience. Even our leaders sometimes succumb. All through our political and economic life are evidences of the virus of immediacy. We forget that the course of civilization has been one long struggle to recog-

56

nize the greater wisdom and efficiency of doing things in roundabout ways that are ultimately timesaving but initially time-consuming. Our universities, like our social institutions, suffer at times from too great outside insistence upon quick, practical results. Thus another external force is added to those which make it difficult for the university, even when its vision is clear, to adhere strictly to its fundamental purpose.

Additional factors, stemming from within the university, impede the ample cultivation of intellectual interests. Perhaps the most obvious of these is the vocationalism to which I have already alluded. Young people are quite naturally interested in getting ready to earn a living. This to them ordinarily means specific training for some designated occupation. It is hard for them to believe that their occupational prospects are not enhanced by specific training in job techniques; it is difficult, if not impossible, for many of them to accept the principle that the best preparation for a given occupation may be general training designed to increase less-specialized skills and abilities, and that the largest growth of intellectual power they can individually achieve is the largest vocational asset they can possibly acquire.

Most of the colleges and schools of Cornell are vocational in character. Thus we have the Engineering College, the College of Architecture, the College of Agriculture, the College of Home Economics, the College of Veterinary Medicine, the Law School, the Medical College. That these units are openly vocational implies no inferiority of position: sound training for a worthy vocational career is one of the most valuable services the university can render. But if the university is to engage in vocational education it should do so in ways becoming an institution of higher learning, devoted basically to the intellectual life. This involves recognition of

57

at least three governing principles: (1) an emphasis upon fundamental disciplines, as distinguished from immediately applicable, narrowly conceived, practical techniques; (2) a sustained pursuit, through scholarly and scientific research, of new knowledge within the field of the vocational art; and (3) a steadfast recognition of the broader implications and social obligations of the vocation for which training is being provided. This is all tantamount to saying that vocational education at the university level should be essentially professional in character. It should, moreover, have a substantial cultural content. Soundly conducted professional education, rightly conceived, need involve no conflict with the primacy of the university's intellectual function.

What of the colleges and schools in our various universities that disclaim any direct vocational or professional aim, as, for example, the college of arts and sciences? It is in these institutions and in our independent liberal arts colleges that we may reasonably look for evidence of the intellectual life at its undergraduate best. What, in fact, do we find?

The situation varies considerably from institution to institution, from subject to subject, from student to student, and notably from professor to professor. However, it is safe to say that upon the whole the situation is far from satisfactory. Even in those colleges, in which the invading forces of vocationalism have been most effectively checked, the intellectual life is not generally promoted with clear success. Certain defects persistently characterize the scholarly work of these institutions.

The chief of these defects I venture to enumerate as follows: (1) the work of the student as organized in a series of formal courses tends to be disjointed and atomistic and lacking in cumulative or additive effect; (2) the instructional

58

outcomes are too largely informational in character; not enough attention is devoted to the development of skills; (3) the results to a regrettable extent prove to be ephemeral; (4) the quality of student interest and effort is in general unsatisfactory; a cult of campus indifference tends to stifle student enthusiasm for things intellectual; (5) the undergraduate experiences of the student do not sufficiently induce lasting habits of self-education; and (6) the results of liberal arts education are commonly lacking in social consequence.

Lest the citation of these deficiences be thought to constitute an overwhelming indictment of what we now have in our undergraduate colleges, let me hasten to add two further observations: (1) there are no insuperable obstacles to improvement of the present situation; and (2) in a good many instances steps have already been successfully taken to remedy some of the defects I have noted. Much remains, however, to be done.

This raises questions of ways and means. That the whole matter has to be analyzed in terms of broad educational policy is quite evident. That specific instructional objectives need to be identified and newly implemented seems to me equally clear. Improved procedures and better administration may help in the whole undertaking, but the heart of the problem lies, of course, in direct teacher-student contacts. No substitute has yet been found, or is likely to be found, for the able and inspiring teacher, himself exemplifying in the flesh the rewarding experiences of the intellectual life.

It is characteristic of current discussions of academic life to emphasize the critical importance of freedom. This is natural enough in view of the hysteria which has developed in some quarters with respect to the supposed extent of Communistic influences. Academic freedom in particular is a profoundly important segment of the freedom we associate with American democracy, and must not be allowed to suffer under the tensions which at present pervade our national life.

But one of the risks academicians now run is that the *responsibilities* we have under the freedom we enjoy will not be sufficiently recognized. Essential neutrality with respect to the great issues of our time threatens to become a fatal defect in the life of American institutions of higher learning.

The explanation of this possible deficiency is to be found in the prevailing concept among academicians of the basic purpose of our institutions of higher learning. This purpose is construed to be the provision of what may be described as a fortified shelter within which individual scholars, scientists, and teachers may follow their individual interests without let or hindrance. It has been assumed that out of the interplay of these individual interests will come an over-all institutional influence serving the vital needs of the supporting social order. In our case this order is a free society, hence the emphasis upon academic freedom.

There is a great deal to be said in defense of this position. The untrammeled acquisition and dissemination of truth is an exceedingly important condition of all enduring human progress. But obviously enough, elements of truth are not all of equal importance, and in the kind of world in which we now live the need of enlightenment varies enormously from one aspect of human experience to another. Even if one accepts the disinterested pursuit of truth as the basic purpose of our institutions of higher learning, important issues of institutional policy remain in the selection of the lines along which truth is to be most vigorously pursued. Shall it be, for example, largely with respect to the nature of the physical universe, or more largely the nature of man and the values he must respect if the dignity and worth of the individual are to be adequately protected? And does the state of the world have anything to do with the decision? Questions like these need more attention than they have had from our educational leaders.

Another closely related problem seems to be equally pressing in the world of today. This second problem has to do with the difficulties encountered in any effort to give a clear, positive, moral, and spiritual affirmation to academic life. Certain church-related institutions are committed to this, of course. But nonsectarian institutions tend to become institutionally amoral. At times they appear extraordinarily aloof from the conflicts of contemporary society.

Some would contend that this is an inevitable consequence of all-out provisions for the disinterested pursuit of truth. I would myself challenge any such conclusion. There are intellectual and moral correlatives to the disinterested pursuit of truth which have not yet been sufficiently recognized. The truth seeker is expected to exhibit an open mind, highly receptive to evidence, a habitual suspension of judgment until dependable evidence is in hand, a tolerance for honest differences of opinion, a stout resistance to bigotry or fanaticism. His should be a mind capable of sustained, calm, critical, reflective, and imaginative thinking. These are intellectual imperatives for the scholar and scientist in his own field; they should characterize the intellectual activities of scholars and scientists outside their specialties. What is more, every effort should be made to induce these same qualities of mind in all the learners who come to our colleges and universities.

There is a profound mental disturbance in contemporary society. People are troubled, confused, distrustful. More and

61

more they are showing symptoms of hysteria, if not of para-
noia. Now, if ever, is the time for keeping our individual and
collective heads clear and straight. It is one of the important
long-range jobs of our colleges and universities to turn out
men and women who have minds trained and equipped to
meet the exacting intellectual requirements of a world in
ideological conflict.

The *moral* correlatives of complete devotion to the truth
seem to me equally clear. How can a person be a genuine
truth seeker who is not in all connections completely honest
and honorable? How can a true scholar, scientist, or teacher
be wanting in personal integrity? These same traits of character, and others basically related to human relationships in
a democracy, should be an essential part of the product of
general education at all levels. Ways and means of obtaining them by formal education in and out of the classroom
demand more attention than they have had. For freedom
imposes its moral as well as its intellectual imperatives, and
the liberty we have treasured is not likely to be retained without an individual and social discipline of mind and spirit to
which education must contribute with all the power it can
possibly muster.

In the kind of world we now face higher education cannot afford to be neutral with respect to the intellectual,
moral, and spiritual issues of our time. It must do more than
demand freedom. It must act positively in terms of the responsibilities freedom imposes. It must assert a constructive
leadership of its own in thwarting the attack the Communists
are making on the whole intellectual, moral, and spiritual
structure of society.

In doing this, higher education will be exhibiting one of
the major parts of its long-range role in a democratic so-

ciety. It will be making its own special contribution to the preservation of the only sort of life that is worth living—life that is free to achieve and to aspire in peace, with justice, and in good will. It will be the height of national folly if, as a result of any of the emergencies through which we are bound to pass, or for sheer lack of national vision, these vitally important long-range services of higher education are in any way impaired or impeded.

To recapitulate: the long-range role of higher education is in two parts. First, the training of specialists. This the colleges and universities have amply demonstrated they can do and do well, given the requisite personnel. Second, the education of intellectual and moral leaders, and the exertion of the sort of institutional influences which such an educational program demands. Along this line goals have not been clearly enough defined, nor ways and means sufficiently devised. But this second task is inescapable if higher education is to measure up to its responsibilities in a world in intellectual, moral, and spiritual conflict.

Emergencies may come and go, but in our time the crisis will not pass. In meeting it, higher education has a long-range role of supreme importance. It is a time for educational as well as other kinds of mobilization. It is a time for commitment as well. For there are battles ahead for higher education if in the world we now face the long-range role of higher education is to be played successfully.

Education for Practical, Social,

and Moral Intelligence

THE over-all responsibility of education in a free society is to raise the level of the people's intelligence. In other words, education must undertake to give the members of a free society an adequate understanding of essential goals and the means of their attainment. The intelligence requisite to the fulfillment of this over-all purpose is of three kinds: (1) practical intelligence; (2) social intelligence; and (3) moral intelligence. These three are in no sense substitutes for one another. Despite the fact that they have been commonly in competition with each other, they are in no way necessarily in conflict. They are, in fact, when fully understood, essentially complementary.

Practical education has to do with the means by which we manage our day-to-day practical affairs. Some practical education is, of course, vocational, but much of it is of broader significance. Thus, instruction in the arts of elementary reading and writing is practical education. While command of these arts may be required in a great many jobs, we can hardly view work on the three R's as primarily vocational in character. At the same time, it is obviously very practical. In general, practical education looks toward the

64

acquisition of specific skills, or the inculcation of designated habits. Civilization of the technical sort we have in America today could not exist without a vast range of practical education.

Social education has to do with our ways of carrying on in large social groups. The most important of these are the governmental. More and more, our individual interests are affected by far-reaching social forces. More and more, we must act in concert if our action is to produce the required results. More and more, it becomes evident that, without social intelligence, we do not have a chance of getting such concerted action under any democratic regime. The social intelligence we must bring to bear relates to all sorts of economic, social and political problems that crowd in on us on every hand—problems of prices and wages, and so of price control and inflation, of taxation and public indebtedness, of tariffs and all sorts of trade regulations, of local government and federal-state relationships, of social suppressions and race relations, of united nations and world order—in short, of all sorts of vast matters which can be brought under control only by wise and farsighted social action. The need of social intelligence, and of education directed toward the attainment of such intelligence, was never quite so striking as it is at this time.

Moral education has to do with the *kind* of life we intend to lead. Fundamentally, this is a matter of attitudes and ideals, of hopes and aspirations, of beliefs and irreducible faith. Stated in other terms, it is a question of what scale of values we bring to bear in deciding individually and collectively what we shall endeavor to make of life. If our practical affairs and social actions are to have order and direction, they must be subject to great governing principles. Moral

65

education undertakes to bring these principles into the open, and through all available means to make them operative.

The differences among practical, social, and moral intelligence, and among the varieties of education directed toward their attainment, can best be seen if we take concrete examples. This might be done in terms of the total educational system in America, or in terms of our higher education alone. I propose, however, to use an even smaller, though no less important, screen upon which to throw the picture.

Nowhere in America today are the lessons of democratic education, past, present and future, more fully exposed than they are in the land-grant colleges and universities.

Looking backward, it is clear that the Morrill Act of 1862 was in its educational provisions an expression of educational revolt. This revolt was on three fronts: First, it sought equality of academic status for the newer disciplines, such as the modern literatures, the social studies, and especially the sciences. Second, it sought recognition of the importance in education of practical and applied subject-matter. Third, it sought wider and more truly democratic opportunities in higher education. The new institutions founded under the act strove to fulfill these requirements. Older institutions in time gave ground. The state universities, partly under the stimulus of the land-grant movement, gathered strength. In time the educational revolt of the middle nineteenth century acquired irresistible momentum. In consequence the contributions of these land-grant institutions to American higher education became immeasurably significant. Let us, therefore, take a closer look at the work they have done.

It was toward practical education that the work of the land-grant colleges was initially directed, and it is in the area of the practical arts that they have made their most notable contributions. By the very provisions of the basic act, they were charged with a primary concern for such branches of learning as were related to agriculture and the mechanic arts, and, with a few exceptions, their early drive was toward these particular interests. For a while it looked as if the mechanic arts would offer better opportunities for effective educational development, but, by the opening of the twentieth century, it was clear that the agricultural arts would be even more successfully pursued in these new-type institutions. The reasons for this somewhat delayed ascendency of agriculture over engineering in the land-grant colleges are complex and need not detain us here. Suffice it to say that in agricultural education and research a demonstration was made in these land-grant institutions of practical education at its best.

In saying this, I have in mind the three-pronged program that was finally evolved. This consisted of soundly conceived and closely articulated activities in resident instruction, extension, and research. Problems in the field of practical farming were carried into the experiment stations and research laboratories for solution. The answers found by those engaged in research and experimentation were promptly conveyed into the field through extension and to the students in training through resident instruction. Farmers in every state in the Union came to look upon the work of the land-grant institutions as genuinely serving their practical needs. And students in the land-grant institutions came to have a full understanding of the inter-relationships of resident instruction, research, and extension.

It is my opinion that the land-grant institutions in this three-pronged program have more successfully demonstrated the values of practical education than has been done in any other phase of higher education in America. It would be greatly to the advantage of the American people if similarly related activities in education and research could be developed in other broad àreas of practical concern. In general, it may be concluded that practical intelligence can be obtained through soundly-organized practical education, and that large social returns are to be had through formal education of this sort. Certainly the land-grant institutions can fairly stand on the record so far as their responsibilities have related to practical education.

There is a disposition in some quarters to view practical education condescendingly. There are those who would deny such education any place in the tradition of liberal education, at any rate at the college level. Such an attitude reflects a failure to appreciate the values that lie in practical education when wisely conceived and effectively conducted. It is good for people to acquire and practice difficult skills. Self-discipline is quite as likely to be cultivated in the plying of an art or the pursuit of a productive endeavor, on one's regular job, as in other phases of human experience. Work can be made to have highly important therapeutic and moral effects, and education which is wisely vocational in design can be very important socially as well as individually. It is when practical education gets in the way of social and moral education that it may need to be curbed. In principle practical education is a primary and indispensable segment of total education in a free society. This the work of the land-grant institutions has fully demonstrated.

Social education is a more difficult undertaking, and in these days one needing much more attention than it has had. The accomplishments of the land-grant institutions in this field have not been so impressive. This is true despite the

68

fact that it has become increasingly clear that practical education will not suffice, even in a field as practical as farming. For the problems of profitable farming have ceased to be primarily problems of individual husbandry. More and more they have become problems of dealing wisely with forces of a wide social character. Commodity surpluses, acreage restrictions, tariff policies, reciprocal trade agreements, foreign markets, monetary policies, debt adjustments, industrial developments—these and many other factors have made the operations of the individual farmer less and less a matter of efficient production and more and more a matter of successful marketing. The corn grower who in the early 1930's found it cheaper to use corn for fuel than to buy coal was not likely to be much interested in learning how to raise corn even more cheaply. The farmer who during the recent war period was not able to get labor with which to harvest his crop of snap beans was not likely to be interested for the time being in learning how to raise more snap beans per acre. As our economic life becomes more and more socialized, the technology of production becomes more and more subordinated to the techniques of successful adjustment to the entire national economy.

This fact has been increasingly recognized in the work of the land-grant institutions, and sustained efforts have already been made to introduce in the work of resident instruction, research, and extension adequate consideration of some of the technical problems involved in the far-flung distribution of agricultural products. This expansion of educational and research activities into the complex social field inevitably encounters serious difficulties, and thus far the progress made in the agricultural colleges in dealing effectively with these larger problems is not too encouraging. The fact remains that responsibility for expansion of the work in agriculture in these directions is now clearly recognized in most important quarters. We may, therefore, expect significant developments along this line in the course of the next few years.

Even if such developments are successfully staged, however, the responsibilities of the land-grant institutions for social education will not be discharged. For the range of social intelligence which we must have is not confined to issues relating to any particular branch of economic activity, such as agriculture. What we have to do in formal education is to reach out into other large problems of contemporary society, such as those of national defense, international and inter-racial relations, minimum civic responsibility as it bears upon the efficiency of our governmental operations at all levels. The time has come when the United States cannot get along without comprehensive social policies, clearly formulated, widely understood, and generally supported by the American people. This calls for a great extension of the work of the colleges and universities of the country in the field of social education. The work that has been done along this line is quite inadequate. In correcting these present deficiencies the colleges and universities of the country have an opportunity and an obligation of surpassing importance. It is hardly conceivable that we can carry on successfully under our established political and economic institutions unless we make great strides soon in the social education of the whole American people.

If this is true of social education, it is even more true of moral education. In this area the shortcomings of present formal education are striking, if not actually shocking. Formal public education in the United States has given relatively slight attention to the development of moral in-

70

telligence. There has been a disposition in many quarters to say that this is not a responsibility of formal education, or that moral intelligence cannot be had by means of formal education. This, however, does not appear to have been the view of the leaders of American thought in the early days of our Federal Government, for in the Northwest Ordinance of 1787 there appears this provision: "Religion, morality, and knowledge being necessary to good government and the happiness of mankind, schools and the means of education shall for all be encouraged." Here religion and morality, as well as knowledge, are made a direct charge to the educational system of the country. I am myself convinced that, unless this charge is accepted by formal education, we have little chance of developing the moral intelligence essential to our survival as a free people. For practical education and social education cannot be fundamentally shaped and directed except as the nature of the good life and the nature of the good state are clearly discerned and become matters of firm and prevailing acceptance. Without faith the people perish. If we are to face life with resolution we must believe that it has meaning. There is no defeat as certain as that springing from a sheer emptiness of experience. As a free people we have no alternative but to declare and live by the faith that is in us.

Given liberty, and educational opportunity, and the right to vote, and all the powers that science and technology can convey, we still face the problem of what we choose to make of life. We cannot get along without a fundamental faith by which to order and direct our strivings. This is true of each of us individually; it is true of all of us as a great, self-governing people. For the great concentrations of power we have developed, economically, politically, and socially make it quite apparent that we can no longer assume that the inter-play of selfish interests will automatically fuse in a serving of the public good. Power politics can wreck us domestically as well as internationally. More and more the fact stares us in the face: we cannot hope to survive as a free people ex-cept as we develop a pervasive sense of responsibility.

The inculcation of a faith is an inescapable responsibility of education. In this responsibility formal education shares. The colleges and universities of the country, including the land-grant colleges, are not now discharging this respon-sibility. The task is doubtless a very difficult one. It will en-tail resort to all sorts of procedures, many of them lying outside the classroom. The fundamental point is that the stakes involved are so great that no effort should be spared, however great may be the investment of time, thought, and money that may prove necessary.

Human affairs have come to a critical juncture. Two world wars and the atomic bomb have produced a world situation in which the outlook of the free peoples of the world hangs in the balance. If the balance is to be swung toward order and peace, justice and prosperity, good will and brotherhood among men, an intellectual, moral and spiritual revolution must be staged.

These three types of education—practical, social, and moral—must be provided at all levels. A fully developed system will spread all the way from elementary schooling to adult education. It will cover everything from local school systems—carrying ultimately through the junior college—to outstanding institutions for advanced training. It must be conceived in terms of a great network encompassing the life of all the people.

In all its reaches education must have the understanding

and appreciation and support of all classes and conditions of men, for the relationships of education to the life of the community are essentially two-way relationships: education must serve the known needs of the community, and in turn must widen and elevate the conception of needs which the community holds.

It is through education, broadly conceived, that knowledge and understanding are spread, skills and habits are attained, attitudes and ideals are established. It is to education, broadly conceived, that we must look for the shaping of the mind and heart of mankind. Herein lies our one best hope for the destiny of our civilization.

A generation ago H. G. Wells issued one of his arresting pronouncements. He drew from his amazingly wide and penetrating studies and observations this sweeping generalization: "Human history becomes more and more a race between education and catastrophe." If this conclusion was warranted after World War I, how much more is it inescapable today. Now that mankind has in its possession the incredible power of atomic energy, how can anyone believe that physical force can any longer be offset with physical force? If anything was ever clear, it is that the future of mankind lies in the realm of mind and spirit rather than of body and brute power. It is through education in all its varied forms that the mind and spirit of man has to be shaped to meet the requirements of the atomic world into which we have now entered. For the free peoples of this world an effective mobilization of all available educational resources is indispensable. It is toward this end that statesmen, as well as educators, must now devote all the resources of thought and courage and vision they can possibly bring to bear.

The Need to Reorient

Liberal Education

THANKS to the phenomenal achievements of physical science, education has today an unprecedented significance. No longer can we entertain the idea that the physical powers in the possession of mankind can be kept under control through a system of physical checks and balances. Any such idea went out as the atomic world came in. It will be only as we succeed in rallying new forces of rational and human living that civilization can hope to survive. More clearly than ever before we can now see that human destiny is going to be an issue of heart and mind, not of matter. That puts education in the very center of our prospects, for how are the heart and mind of mankind to be shaped save through the influences of education, broadly conceived?

I say "education, broadly conceived" because the task of shaping the heart and mind of mankind obviously extends far beyond the bounds of formal instruction. The home, the church, the press, the theater, the motion picture, the radio and television, the periodical, the opinion molder, and the leader in every walk of life—all these and more share in the responsibilities that now are upon us. Any undertaking to weld such diverse influences into a common effort for good

74

would seem manifestly impossible if the world were today what it was yesterday. But obviously it is not. The bomb that dropped on Hiroshima made the world for all time profoundly different. Beyond any possibility of doubt, human affairs have now to be given a new order and direction. The old-style play of self-seeking interests can only end in universal disaster. Only in an intellectual, moral, and spiritual revolution can we hope to be saved.

Clearly enough, what we most need at the moment in wise educational planning for the future is a set of governing principles. These principles need to be formulated in terms of both future and past.

For generations prior to the middle of the nineteenth century liberal education at the college level maintained a united front in a curriculum devoted largely to philosophy, mathematics, and the classics. Over a long period of educational expansion, this curriculum served its purposes well. It gave results of unmistakable value. It was never seriously challenged. But between 1850 and 1900 the solid front of the traditional curriculum was completely broken by social and cultural forces of great power. Among these forces, three were decisive: (1) the intellectual awakening; (2) the rise of the industrial classes; and (3) the spread of science and technology.

The intellectual awakening, starting in the Renaissance and rising rapidly thereafter, produced some of its most striking results early in the nineteenth century. In the field of formal education at the college level it led to a spectacular penetration of the traditional curriculum by the newer disciplines: by modern languages and literatures, history and the social studies, and especially the natural sciences. Generally speaking, the barriers which had for centuries confined

75

the intellectual interests of mankind were demolished for all time. Nothing could have unsettled more completely the traditional classical curriculum in which liberal education had so long and successfully maintained its offering.

The second great force stemmed from the rise of the industrial classes. Before the nineteenth century liberal education was regarded as the privilege of those preparing for one of the established professions. Farmers and mechanics, artisans and laborers were not expected to aspire to formal education at the college level. But the second quarter of the nineteenth century brought insistent demands from these less-privileged classes that they be provided with more extended educational opportunities. In this country the most striking result of this agitation was the passage of the Morrill Act of 1862, making provision for the establishment of a land-grant college in each of the several states and territories. These new institutions were founded to provide instruction, especially in agriculture and the mechanic arts, to meet the educational needs of the so-called industrial classes. The practical arts were to be brought within the scope of higher education, and higher education in general made a more common experience of all classes of society. Here was another fundamental challenge to the traditional liberal arts curriculum. It was a challenge which ultimately had a sharply disruptive effect.

The third and most pervasive force that impinged upon traditional liberal education during the nineteenth century was the rapidly mounting prestige and influence of science and technology. The consequences which flowed from this particular development were in no wise confined to formal education. They permeated the life of the people from top to bottom. They not only directly affected the ·material base

76

of modern society; they deeply influenced the thought and aspirations of all classes and conditions of mankind. They gave rise to a form of materialism which has been the most striking feature of the cultural and philosophical outlook of contemporary society. They profoundly affected the interests and activities of all of the established social institutions, and radically changed the outlook and operations of formal education at all levels. For traditional liberal education, this rapid spread of science and technology was the most disruptive influence of all.

The combined impact on liberal education of these three great movements proved to be devastating. The traditional curriculum collapsed. The united front previously maintained by the liberal arts colleges was shattered, and a disorderly retreat ensued. The simultaneous introduction of the elective system added further to the rout. Educational disorder became a characteristic of the times.

It was in this state of widespread educational confusion that certain invading forces asserted themselves. One of the most important of these was systematic research, especially of the scientific type. This was closely connected with the general spread of science and technology. The extraordinary advances made in this field gave experimental and investigative work an irresistible prestige. Undergraduate colleges fell under the spell of the graduate schools of the country, especially as the latter were brought, during the second half of the nineteenth century, under the influence of the German universities. In due course education came to be regarded as most respectable when attached to research, and research in turn was least open to challenge when it followed the lead of laboratory techniques. Even in those fields in which quite a different set of intellectual goals might have been expected

77

to prevail—as, for example, in literature, philosophy and the fine arts—the powerful influence of experimental science, with its emphasis upon factual data and precise measurement, became all too evident. The net effect of all this was a temporary destruction of many of the most important values residing in the liberal arts.

Associated with this encroachment of research was a tendency to high specialization. This was in some respects inevitable, since research gets its results most effectively when it is directed toward narrowly circumscribed phenomena. Thus, emphasis upon research may be said to lead inevitably to a high degree of specialization. Consequently, for some time past we have witnessed a tendency for the total field of knowledge to become more and more fragmented. The subdivisions of the total curriculum have tended to become more and more numerous; and the specialists, in consequence, have tended to become less and less acquainted with fields other than their own. Over-all integration has become increasingly difficult. For the time being at least, the unity of the liberal arts curriculum has largely disappeared.

The invasion of higher education by the so-called industrial classes gave rise to excesses of another sort. Undue emphasis came to be placed on practical considerations, particularly those of vocational relevance. Quick and easy applications of the outcomes of instruction were sought. This immediacy of objective had many unfortunate effects. After all, investments in education cannot wisely be expected to pay dividends at once. Practical aims in education need to be conceived in broad and enduring terms. Too much of education of late has been arranged to get quick returns.

This spread of shortsighted vocationalism was in some ways only a manifestation of a broader movement in which

78

much of formal education came to stress individual interests at the expense of social objectives. It is all very well for education to be so designed as to serve the particular concerns of the individual learner, but at bottom education is an instrument of social policy and must be made to serve social ends. In the disorder which prevailed in liberal education after the turn of the century, altogether too little attention was paid to the social purposes which education must be made to serve.

The lack of compelling educational interests during this period of confusion set the stage for still another invasion, which has given to higher education in this country during the past half-century some of its most striking features. The forces of administration have come to play a larger and larger part in the direction of the affairs of higher education. Phenomenal developments of plant have occurred. Extracurricular programs have been greatly expanded. Intercollegiate athletics, in particular, have developed a following which has threatened the normal balance of American academic life. Many of these expansions of plant and program have been all to the good; in fact, thoroughly sound, even when appraised from a strictly academic point of view. On the other hand, there have been many instances in which the developments have hampered, if not actually obstructed, the progress of the educational enterprise. In so far as these excesses have occurred, they may fairly be charged to the failure of liberal education for a time to have any clear and adequate conception of its own important function.

To sum up: Liberal education in this country during recent decades has been in a sad state of disorder. Having lost its earlier strength, it has been pushed about by forces of a more or less hostile character. Prompt rehabilitation is greatly

79

to be desired. To effect this, a general overhauling would seem to be essential. We can undertake to suggest some of the lines along which the necessary realignment of the forces of liberal education must be accomplished. I shall briefly touch upon seven of these.

(1) It is clear that liberal education must be freed of the shackles which have been placed upon it by the forces of scientific research. The obligations of those charged with responsibility for liberal education are not identical with those responsible for the advancement of knowledge. Both are exceedingly important in academic life. Each has its special place. The two need not be in conflict. However, it is of the utmost importance that they be wisely co-ordinated. The point I make is that liberal education must not be subject to any dictation or domination by research. That does not mean that research should be given any diminished stature, but rather that the fundamental purposes of liberal education must be given freer play. The idea that liberal education in a free society is a function of primary importance must be stoutly defended. In fact, the social values that reside in liberal education are of such vast importance that they must be specifically serviced by all the resources we can bring to bear.

(2) It follows that the tendency to excessive specialization, which has plagued college education in this country for decades, must be broken. We are desperately in need of a new synthesis in liberal education—a synthesis which will work a sound combination of the contributions made by the narrower disciplines. Excesses of departmentalization constitute one of the chronic weaknesses of the current academic organization. To offset this, the broad purposes of liberal education must be carefully identified, and then translated

80

into specific objectives toward which teaching materials and methods can be skillfully directed.

(3) This points to another consideration of unrecognized importance; namely, the necessity of keeping the entire educative process under continuous evaluation. There has been altogether too little specification of the goals of instruction in liberal education and too little close appraisal of the relative effectiveness of different ways and means of attaining these goals. In promoting liberal education we must have means of telling what is effectual and what is not. In other words, success and failure must be made distinguishable, and adequate evaluation must become an essential part of the total process. Liberal education has lived too long on its reputation. It is time it undertook to regain its prestige through renewed demonstration of specific educational achievements.

(4) As objectives are probed and results appraised, it will become clear that liberal education cannot afford to neglect or to subordinate to other ends the promotion of the intellectual life. This does not mean that the values of extracurricular experience can be wisely neglected. College students need to live what they learn. The whole person has to be developed. But this is likely to be accomplished only as the core of campus activities is an assiduous cultivation of the powers of the mind. In this basic undertaking emphasis needs to be placed upon specific skills rather than upon essential bodies of knowledge, though both skill and knowledge should appear in the end results. Men and women on the college campus should be led to learn how knowledge is gained and wisdom won. They should, through practice, improve their command of the difficult art of critical thinking. They should come to know something of the nature of imaginative and

81

creative thought. They should learn what it means to abide with reason. They should strive for intelligence. They should acquire a love of truth and a firsthand acquaintance of what it means to pursue truth disinterestedly. In all these endeavors, they should master skills, acquire habits, and project ideals which will make them worthy of the freedom they enjoy. There are no substitutes for these purposes in the undertakings of liberal education.

(5) If the pursuit of the intellectual life is to be successful, every effort must be made to enlist the interest of learners and to cultivate their appreciation of the learning process. At this point the insistence of the progressives has been fundamentally sound. There is much to be gained and nothing lost in packing as much meaning as possible into the materials and methods through which the student is led to learn. It would appear that, if the interests of the students are to be satisfactorily met, some functional reorganization of the subject matter of the liberal arts curriculum may be necessary, but this need involve no relaxation of the rigorous training of the mind, which is of the very essence of liberal education. There need be nothing soft about the idea of giving learners some appreciation of the full meaning and significance of what they are called upon to do. It is too much to ask of students that they take the purposes of liberal education largely on faith.

(6) The interests of students are certain to look in part toward the future job or profession. This is quite as it should be. Work has a contribution to make to satisfaction in life which is not nowadays sufficiently recognized. Forward-looking education, in the provision of educational opportunity, cannot afford to look upon vocational purposes as essentially inferior. There is, in fact, no reason why liberal

82

education itself should not service important vocational interests. The current tendency to set vocational and liberal education in opposition to one another is not only a mistake but one that has highly unfortunate effects. So far as the different phases of formal education are concerned, it is of the utmost importance to fuse in single programs the economic, social, and personal needs of the students, from whatever class or circumstance they may come. This will entail important changes in outlook and method for both liberal and vocational education.

(7) Finally, it is important to recognize that liberal education is never going to accomplish its purposes except as it becomes a part, though a very important part, of a comprehensive and unified system of education, democratically organized and democratically patronized from top to bottom. In this over-all system adult education must have a significant part, and liberal education must be in part adult education. Liberal education is unsound education if it becomes class education. This does not mean that it need be open to all comers in its upper reaches; there may well be a selection of talent. But the ideals of liberal education should not be reserved for the upper ranges of education; they should be introduced at all levels and for all classes. What we need is an overhauling, not only of liberal education at the college level, but of other parts of education as well, with a view to the ordering of a complete system, carefully and wisely devised to achieve stated social ends. Education, like all other important social undertakings, needs to have explicitly set goals—goals dependable and adequate. It is against such clearly stated goals that the entire structure and activity of American education must be consistently operated.

The responsibilities facing education in these critical times cannot be discharged by piecemeal measures. Great social purposes can be adequately served only by great social means. We cannot get along in the world of today without effective education for civic responsibilities, for social discipline, for national defense, for cultural unity, and for international understanding. It is in support of an improved social order that the full strength of education at all levels and of all types must be promptly rallied.

Science, Social Progress,

and Higher Education

ON A recipe written largely by the liberal movement of the last two centuries, modern man has mixed an exceedingly potent brew. We may call it "Freemen's Punch." The chief ingredients of this brew are three: science and technology; mass education; and universal suffrage. The mixture of these three has given modern man a thrilling experience. He has felt uplifted and has "gone places." The fact remains that he is beginning to have doubts with regard to some phases of the experience. He is beginning to wonder whether the experience does not in some respects resemble a case of intoxication. Certainly right now man is confused. He has lost his sense of direction. He has, moreover, developed a terrible headache. Apparently something is wrong with this "Freemen's Punch." Obviously, as it has been mixed, it has aftereffects which are very disturbing. The recipe would seem to need changing.

The dictators have found this out and have taken prompt action. They have changed the recipe radically. They have, in the first place, raised the proportion of science and technology. They have simultaneously reduced and considerably modified that part of the brew which consists of universal suffrage. They have added a new element; namely, a cunningly devised and consistently applied official treachery; and they have also mixed in a substantial portion of still another ingredient, a clearly formulated and rigorously observed, comprehensive national policy. The new combination they have worked out has proved to be terrific in its immediate effects. It threatens to put free society into a permanent stupor. It has developed a quick potency substantially greater than that of the punch mixed by free men during the past two centuries.

Free men face the problem of what they are going to do with the recipe they have been using in "Freemen's Punch." Something is obviously wrong with it. A brew of the three elements alone—science and technology, mass education, and universal suffrage—clearly does not produce the right kind of experience for mankind.

This raises the direct question: What experience after all should be sought by a free society? In other words: What are the goals toward which mankind should be striving?

Despite the fact that the best minds of all times have wrestled with the problem, there have always been wide differences of view with regard to the nature of human progress.

Many are prone to think of progress in terms of large increases of material goods and services. However, if anything is writ clear on the pages of history, it is that human happiness and well-being are not to be had securely from an abundance of physical possessions. Of course, some present increase of physical goods and services is indispensable. We must have such a supply of goods and service as will assure health, provide for a minimum decency of living for humankind, provide substantial security, and remove an ever-pressing sense of fear. We must provide these bare essentials if we are going to establish a free society in which there is real opportunity for self-realization. What we must really drive at is to rid mankind of slavery. We must strive for human relationships that are essentially sympathetic and considerate. We must find ways of giving man an enduring sense of meaning in life. We must provide all this in a setting of peace. Certainly all these are indispensable elements in any wisely conceived human progress.

Suppose we impose these elementary notions of human progress on the experience of mankind over the last two centuries during which mankind has been partaking of "Freemen's Punch." Let us re-examine the ingredients of that punch in the light of the nature of human progress.

Far and away the most important of the active elements in our great liberal tradition is the pursuit of truth under the leadership of science and technology. If there is anything that characterizes our present age, it is the pre-eminence of science. Science is our miracle worker. It is to science that we look for relief from practically all our ills. It has transformed our ways of life. Within our own individual memories it has performed incredible wonders. In a sense it is what we have come to worship. It has a prestige in modern society equaled by nothing else. In more ways than one, science has taken possession of us. It has come to rule us with an iron hand.

This being so, it is of the utmost importance that we examine closely the impact of science on society. The first point to make in that connection is that science is totally indifferent toward society. Science as science has no consideration for human values, nor for the social order. As was observed by Veblen, "Science knows no policy, no utility, no

87

better or worse." Science performs its wonders irrespective of what they do to us. It is constantly working on society totally unpremeditated and totally unpredicted consequences.

Take a very simple example, perhaps hardly within the range of science, but certainly akin to science and technology: the invention by James Hargreaves of the spinning jenny. This rudimentary device, which enabled one spinner to spin eight or ten threads instead of one, initiated the factory system in England. In the course of time it led to the complete transformation of the organization of industrial enterprise. It was one of the first signs of oncoming industrialism. Did James Hargreaves, when he developed his jenny, have any notion of what he was doing to mankind? The answer is obviously no, not the slightest inkling.

Take a more recent example—the modern gas engine. Did those ingenious inventors who first brought the gas engine into effective form have any appreciation of what that instrument was going to do to modern society? Just as clearly the answer is no. As a matter of fact the impact of the gas engine upon society is still to be completely discerned. We do know that it has profoundly changed modern man's outlook and experience. But the inventors of the gas engine did not see all this.

We have to conclude that science performs its wonders without any serious reference to what those wonders are going to do to human progress. However much human progress may depend upon the knowledge which science alone can supply, it is perfectly clear that science alone gives no guaranty whatever of human progress. That being so, we cannot avoid some consideration of what science actually does to us.

88

Let me sketch in barest outline the nature of the contributions of science viewed from the angle of the effects of science on society. From this point of view, we may profitably think of the contributions of science as falling into five fairly distinct groupings.

In the first place, there are those contributions of science which give us understanding of the laws of nature, and some ability to forecast natural events even in areas in which we cannot possibly control nature. The field of astronomy is perhaps the most outstanding example of this. The eclipse of the sun no longer terrifies man. He knows how it happens. He can predict it with nicety. Some of the most important contributions of science are of this character.

Somewhat akin to this first type of contribution of science are those which permit man to intervene in natural process and in a measure to effect control, though perhaps a limited control, the natural process remaining substantially as it was. The most striking example of this type of contribution is birth control. There are widely variant scientific contributions which are of this general character. They impinge deeply upon our thought and action.

A third group of scientific contributions takes the form of release of the tremendous energies that lie in the physical universe. Possibly the most far-reaching contributions of science are of this sort. They have led to a virtual freeing of man from the necessity of applying himself with a view to providing sheer physical force. Mankind has now really been largely released from the necessity of providing energy or force.

Another distinctive category of scientific contribution has to do with the supply of new and previously unknown materials. We get striking examples of that nowadays, principally as a result of the advances of modern industrial chemistry. Not only are previously unknown materials supplied; materials previously known but inadequately supplied are sometimes rendered profusely abundant.

Finally and perhaps as striking as any other form are the contributions of science which have annihilated space. These are the contributions which move us about from place to place with incredible speed and ease; and those further contributions in the field of communication which bring to us instantly, or almost so, sounds and sights originating afar.

Roughly, then, the contributions of science, in so far as they relate to their impact on society, fall into these five categories. Let us now look at those different types of scientific contribution with a view to glimpsing the nature of their impact on mankind.

Take the first two, those which have given us extraordinary understanding of natural law and some ability to intervene and to redirect vital processes. The impact of science in this particular form has been most pronounced in the changes that have been wrought in our over-all view of the universe, or in our philosophy of life. Our scheme of moral values has been profoundly affected. We have come to understand nature to such an extent that not uncommonly we think of it as sheer mechanism, as something that is purely material in essence. Almost inevitably the popular mind has, in this connection, developed an attitude of skepticism, an outlook which is primarily materialistic. Its sense of moral and spiritual values has been substantially impaired, and the hold which established religion has had on man's thinking has been greatly weakened. This particular impact of science on life is of immeasurable significance. We are not yet fully aware of what has happened to us along this line. We do know that the basis of human relationships has been profoundly affected.

Let us turn next to two of the other categories of scientific contribution: those relating to the release of physical energy, and those providing for the supply of previously unknown or previously scarce materials. The impact of science in these two categories has been most conspicuous in the field of economics. Our productive arrangements for turning out the goods and services necessary for the sustenance of society have been turned inside out and upside down as a result of science and technology. The innovations started in England two hundred years ago are still working out their effects. In consequence we now live in an age of urbanized industrialism.

The potency of science and technology along this line is not yet fully realized. The technocrats some few years ago undertook to tell us something of what science and technology could do if given a completely free chance to operate. The story in some respects seemed incredible; yet I am led to believe that the technocrats were substantially correct, that science and technology, freed of all economic restraint, could come very close to doing what the technocrats said science and technology could do—provide for all an abundance of physical goods and services.

That is what science and technology offer us. Why do we not get the plenty that science and technology offer? The answer lies largely in the economic system. The impediments, the apparently insuperable obstacles, lie in an intricate system of prices, values, costs, profits, a capital

91

structure, a system of established property values and rights of all kinds. These have to be protected in some measure if we are not going completely revolutionary.

Science in this area is threatening a conflict which presents one of contemporary society's most serious problems. This conflict increasingly takes the form of property interests *versus* human interests. There is no point at which the profound disturbance through which we are moving comes more clearly into focus than it does in this area where science and technology are impinging on an established economic system.

Take the remaining category of scientific contribution, that which has annihilated space. Where has that had its most conspicuous impact on society? It seems to me that the area in which we can see the changes taking place most rapidly is the area of political organization and procedure. Science's annihilation of space has rapidly outmoded the political organization which came to pass as a result of the liberal movement of the past two centuries. The isolated national state makes no sense with distances gone. Moreover, with our enormously improved techniques of communication, it is quite evident that political processes are destined to undergo marked change. They are in fact already undergoing great changes. What propaganda can do with these modern techniques has been demonstrated abroad; we are getting increasingly acquainted with it at home. When one voice can encircle the globe and address English-speaking people in every land, when the President of the United States on short notice can address some fifty or sixty million listeners simultaneously, we are in a new era politically.

This whole technique of modern communication is large-scale business. It presents problems of regulation and control in the interest of free communication which are totally unprecedented. It opens avenues for political influence, for high-pressuring of all sorts, for the elaboration of stream-lined methods of propaganda, the like of which we have never seen. In short, the impact of science and technology on political organization presents another of the tremendous problems with which modern society is confronted.

So much for a very brief and quite inadequate indication of how science is impinging on modern society; what it is doing to society; and the nature of the problems which it is imposing upon modern man. May we return now to the question of what must be added to the three components of modern liberalism—science and technology, mass educa-tion, and universal suffrage—if human progress is to be assured?

At least two elements must be added to the other three. In the first place, and most obviously, we shall not move along the path of human progress unless we associate with the three elements which have dominated our lives through the past two centuries the element of a restored religious faith and an accompanying firm and effective moral order. There is no way to make a worthy civilization without a posi-tive faith, without a religion which will uplift human motiva-tion, discipline human interest, and give a sense of value and meaning to human experience.

In the second place, it is equally obvious that a fifth in-gredient must be added; namely, a comprehensively con-ceived and vigorously applied social policy. Science gives no direction. Mass education and universal suffrage do not orient society, locate man, or direct his efforts. We must have an over-all charting of the course. The dictators have made that perfectly evident. The enormous increase in the

93

power of their regimes lies in substantial measure in their sense of direction. They think they know where they want to get, and they map programs accordingly. Free society can do no less. We must have our own blueprints. We must have our own firmly established and wisely conceived social policy.

The "Freemen's Punch" of which we have been partaking will not do as it stands. We have sufficient evidence of that. We must change the recipe, not as the dictators have changed it, but with full understanding of the nature of human progress. We must change it by adding these two indispensable ingredients: a positive and inspiriting religious faith, and an adequate, comprehensive social policy.

What of the role of universities in all this? Universities have specific responsibilities in the field of research and education. It is my considered opinion that the colleges and universities will be making a fatal mistake if they move seriously out of this particular province. Education and research do not mix soundly with political action. They should be kept intact. They should preserve their own essential integrity. One of the threats to contemporary free society consists of repeated attempts on the part of political organizations of one sort or another to invade and take possession of the agencies of education and research. We must preserve the fundamental functions of education and research in the life of our educational institutions. We must safeguard them against encroachment.

The colleges and universities of the country must be free to acquire knowledge as they are able, and to disseminate it as best they can. They must not be expected to lend themselves to programs of propaganda, nor made to serve as instruments in the action programs of either government or

94

business. In return they must safeguard, by every possible means, the competence, honesty, fairness, and integrity of the scholars, scientists, and teachers who carry on the work. For the long pull, the untrammeled pursuit of truth in which they engage and the training in critical thinking which they provide must be kept strong, vital, and progressive.

Suppose we succeed in doing that; what, then, of our responsibilities in the field of education and research with reference to the total world situation and the impending re-organization of contemporary social life? I venture to think that even if we move within the confines of education and research, we are under compulsion substantially to revise, or amplify, our programs.

Educators, too, have fallen under the domination of science and technology. The land-grant institutions were launched as the great movement of science and technology into American education began. It happens that one of the leaders in that movement—I am inclined to think that he was perhaps the most important and influential man in that entire movement—was the first President of Cornell; his name was Andrew Dickson White. As one of the educational leaders of his time, he made his great drive against the rigid and complacent classicism of the higher education of that day. He was one of the first, not only to advocate, but actually to introduce the principle of the educational equality of science and the humanities. It was a movement of reform unmistakably needed. Beyond all accounting, we are today the beneficiaries of the educational movement thus initiated. The time has come, however, when our absorption in science and technology must be brought into balance with other fundamental interests and considerations. No longer can educational institutions by-pass the basic moral and religious needs of our time. Neither can they fail to give sustained attention to pressing questions of over-all social policy. The necessity of ministering effectively to these great social needs, which science and technology alone cannot serve, is all too evident. In short, educators must venture into new fields in American higher education. Quite properly and most profitably, we were engrossed for a time in a sustained effort to give society the full benefits of science. In that direction we have accomplished great things. Now, however, we must supplement that effort with equally important endeavors in other directions. The times call for reorientation and redirection of the work of the educational institutions, that they may continue to make their contributions to the just, humane, peaceful, free society in which alone their work will find its ultimate justification.

Competition Between

Teaching and Research

in American Universities

THE text for this paper is taken from the Harvard Committee Report on *Some Problems of Personnel in the Faculty of Arts and Sciences*. Speaking of criteria of faculty selection, the report carries this statement:

Both teaching and research are recognized as criteria because the University is a center where learning is not only advanced but also disseminated through the influence of older upon younger minds. . . .

The University has occasionally created "research professorships," divorced altogether from formal instruction. But normally a member of the Faculty of Arts and Sciences is by profession a teacher. The College and Graduate School are teaching institutions. The man who accepts appointment to their Faculty does so with this understanding. . . . In so far as Harvard seeks to attract the most ambitious and talented students, the University owes these selected individuals teaching of the highest possible order. It becomes the duty of the University in selecting its staff to take account of this exacting requirement. . . . While it is important that Harvard should be a community of scholars, it is also important that the members of its faculties should regard themselves as a community of teachers.

As the text for this paper these statements may sound unpromising. I have to admit that there is nothing about them that is particularly striking, or novel, or even suggestive. In fact the quotations may fairly be regarded as nothing more than a reiteration of a view that has long since become a commonplace in academic discussion in this country. *Of course* both teaching and research are functions of the American university. That much may be taken as axiomatic.

But the significant fact about the text is that it appeared in a notable report of a Harvard faculty committee in the year 1939. The setting of the statements is significant. No American university has more assiduously and successfully promoted the interests of scholarly and scientific research than has Harvard. No American university has more ample means for fostering these research interests than has Harvard. No American university appears to be any more firmly committed to staunch support of the expensive business of scholarly and scientific research than is Harvard. Yet the faculty of Harvard College and the administrative officials of Harvard University have, after thorough-going study, stood by the traditional doctrine that teaching and research are both primary functions of the American university.

For the purposes of this paper it is quite unnecessary to attempt any more definite determination of the relative importance of teaching and research at the university level. It would be easy to contend that, since our American universities are after all educational institutions rather than research institutes, the teaching function is surely the more fundamental. But it will suffice for the analysis I wish to present if the position is taken that teaching and research are essentially co-ordinate functions of the American university; that neither can be wisely subordinated to the other; that certainly no lower status for teaching than for research is to be contemplated. The Harvard committee report appears to take this position for granted. Presumably few if any persons would challenge it.

In the light of this basic principle let us view the American university scene as it has presented itself during recent years. Hazardous as any attempt at generalization may be—and certainly there are notable exceptions to any generalization that may be made—I submit that it becomes increasingly evident that our American universities are being so administered that success in research is going at a definite premium over success in teaching. The competition for men who have made their marks in scholarly and scientific research grows more and more intense—one might almost say ruthless. In speed of recognition, in grade of initial appointment, in rate of promotion, in programing of assigned duties, the man of demonstrated research ability is in a preferred position. With few exceptions the presidents of our universities must view with mixed feelings any notable additions to human knowledge made by members of their staffs; for there is immediate danger of losing these spotlighted scholars and scientists to other institutions whose offers cannot be successfully countered. It is not difficult to see who are the direct beneficiaries of the almost inevitable ensuing competition.

Meanwhile the successful teacher carries on his equally important function without benefit of publicity. Even if it is insisted that in due course his talents will be recognized and his success rewarded, it is clear that his academic progress will be slower. The Harvard committee sought by a questionnaire to ascertain the sources of dissatisfaction among the younger members of the Harvard faculty. After examining the replies, the committee reports:

99

These replies reveal the existence of a belief that teaching, and particularly the tutorial type of teaching, receives inadequate recognition, and that there is an over-insistence on published research, with the result that both teaching and broad scholarship tend to be neglected.

The same belief can be found on virtually every university campus in the country. Upon both a priori and empirical grounds the conclusion is inescapable: under present conditions teaching and research are not *experiencing* equal favor in the work of our American universities.

One of the comfortable ways of dealing administratively with this situation is to belittle the idea that teaching and research are in any way competing functions at the university level. The idea is that teaching and research go hand in hand; that the successful teacher will inevitably be engaged in fruitful research; and the successful scholar or scientist just as surely will be an effective teacher. This proposition in this general form is wishful thinking of the baldest sort. The eminent scholar or scientist who is also an inspiring teacher is, of course, for the university administrator an answer to prayer; but we know all too well that answers to this particular prayer appear in the flesh very infrequently. On this general point, the Harvard committee has this to say:

It is sometimes assumed that teaching will take care of itself, as a sort of by-product; or that while published research is a rare and difficult attainment, almost anybody can teach. Nothing can be further from the truth, and such an assumption can only imply a relaxation of teaching standards.

There has been a lot of loose thinking in university circles with regard to this relationship of teaching and research. Part of the prevailing confusion results from emphasis upon propositions too broad and general to be applicable to the administrative problem with which we are actually faced. No one is going to quarrel seriously with the dictum of the Harvard committee that "between teaching and scholarship there is in principle no conflict whatever, since teaching is a manifestation of scholarship, and scholarship a condition of teaching." But what of the realities with which the young scholar is faced? As the committee goes on immediately to say:

But the actual schedule of teaching may interfere with scholarly development and with professional advancement. This will result when the total volume of teaching, of whatever kind, is so great as to trespass upon the time required for independent study. Of approximately eighty of the younger teachers who testified that they felt a conflict between research and teaching, the great majority referred to this difficulty. Conflict will result when the variety of teaching activities requires a dispersion of attention inconsistent with intellectual continuity and concentration, and in so far as teaching because of its elementary character demands an extensive secondary knowledge that hinders the intensive cultivation of a special field.

In short, teaching and research may in a broad sense be complementary and mutually supporting functions, but they are clearly in the concrete day-to-day duties of the members of a university faculty competing and mutually excluding interests.

Another reason for confusion on this whole subject is failure to distinguish the variant conditions at different levels of instruction. The conflict between teaching and research is barely perceptible, if it appears at all, at the level of the most advanced and specialized studies. As the Harvard committee points out:

101

The specialized field of graduate teaching will ordinarily co-incide with that of the teachers' central intellectual interest. Graduate students and the best undergraduate students are from the standpoint of scholarship often an asset rather than a liability. They become associates, collaborators, critics, or disciples, and afford the opportunity for transmitting an unfinished task or new line of inquiry to later generations.

The situation is strikingly different in the greater part of undergraduate teaching. Here the interests of teaching and research are, from the point of view of faculty members and university alike, essentially in competition.

It does not follow from this that sound lines of develop-ment of faculty personnel must rest upon the principle of extreme specialization, with some members of staff devoting themselves entirely to research and others exclusively to teaching. As a rule it is desirable that all members of staff participate to some extent in both functions. But the pro-portions in which teaching and research are mixed in the duties of individual members of university faculties must and should vary widely—certainly unless or until our universi-ties are converted into institutions for advanced study only. For the present, some members of the university staff will devote themselves largely to research, with strictly limited responsibilities for instruction; others will devote themselves primarily to teaching, with substantially reduced require-ments of scholarly or scientific output. In no other way are the fundamental obligations of the university for *both* teach-ing and research to be fairly, honestly, and efficiently dis-charged.

University administrators find themselves faced with these facts. Our institutions are expected to treat teaching and research as co-ordinate functions. The two functions are

102

in certain important respects essentially competing. The conditions of this competition appear at present to be definitely uneven, the function of research enjoying substantial differential advantages. If teaching and research are to be handled as co-ordinate responsibilities of the university, ways must be devised for equalizing the competition between them.

The present inequalities of the competition between teaching and research derive from a number of factors, but far and away the most important of these is the quick and relatively unequivocal recognition of outstanding achievement in the field of research. Reputation follows promptly upon the publication of the results of scholarly or scientific investigation. Of course, wide differences of appraisal by established workers in the field frequently appear, but the speed with which a newcomer, if he has exceptional ability, especially in the natural sciences, can develop prestige is amazing. Quick appraisal, wide publicity in academic circles, and interinstitutional bidding account for a large share of the differential advantage which research enjoys currently in comparison with teaching.

The competitive weakness of the teacher stems from the fact that his work, even if it is of superior quality, goes largely unheralded. Back of this lies the even more important fact that it goes largely unappraised. Two changes must be brought about if the existing preferential treatment of research in our American universities is to be eliminated, and the co-ordinate rating of teaching and research is to be restored: first, ways and means of appraising teaching must be devised; second, dependable information with regard to teaching ability must gain wider circulation in university and college circles.

I am under no illusions regarding the difficulties that lie

ahead in any systematic attempt to evaluate instruction at the university level. I am familiar with the hostility toward any such idea which exists among a great many of our university and college professors. Among many of these the very thought of any move to bring the effectiveness of teaching under critical examination is anathema. The fact remains that it is the teachers themselves who pay the heavy penalties of the present differential disadvantages of teaching, as contrasted with research, in our American institutions of higher learning. It is the teachers themselves who have most to gain from the development of reliable appraisals of teaching efficiency, and from continuing efforts to improve the effectiveness of the teaching process.

On every campus we encounter the theory which many professors find strangely reassuring, that teaching is a mysterious art, the essence of which can never be known. But the idea that the contrasts between good, bad, and indifferent classroom work cannot be told is patently absurd. We do not hesitate to suggest that individual teachers *in the secondary schools* be observed to find out whether they know how to teach. Of course we do not offer this same proposal with equal readiness in regard to teachers in our liberal arts colleges, but the fact remains that we recognize fully some of the results which flow from good teaching at all levels. We know that the good teacher imparts knowledge. We know that in certain directions he develops skill. We know that the thoroughly successful teacher awakens interest and enthusiasm, affects attitudes and ideals, induces respect for intelligence and appreciation of the better things in life. We know that by his example he induces in his students the good manners of the intellectual world in which he himself lives.

We run the risk of no serious divergence of view as to the

components of good teaching. Most of the controversy relates to the question whether or not we can ever bring them
under observation. That merely raises questions of sound
procedure: How are we going to initiate a concerted attack
on the whole problem in an effort to get tangible results
which can be effectively utilized? The teaching art is undoubtedly a complex one, and it would be a great mistake
to proceed to the evaluation of teaching outcomes except in
terms of a painstaking and slowly evolving program, in
which some of the most important factors will not lend themselves, certainly for the present, to any specific measurement.
Nevertheless, teaching, like other forms of professional practice, is susceptible to analysis, and the essentials of good
teaching are generally recognized, even if efforts to discover
their concrete existence in the work of any university faculty
are strongly resisted.

The important thing is to develop undertakings looking
toward the comprehensive and systematic study of all available means of evaluating instructional outcomes at the different levels and in the different types of educational program.
After all, teaching is already being appraised in a way. Administration finds appraisal unavoidable, even if it has to be
done by the present unsatisfactory catch-as-catch-can methods. Increasingly the undergraduates are making and cir-
culating their own evaluations of the professors and their
classroom offerings, sometimes with devastating and in-
equitable results. The question really is not whether we shall
have appraisals or no appraisals, but rather what appraisals
we shall have and under what auspices.

My own opinion is that any program of comprehensive
and systematic appraisal of teaching is most likely to develop satisfactorily if it is organized under direct control of

105

the teachers themselves. Teaching must cease to be an academic untouchable. For the present, appraisal services may have to be kept optional; but that they should be available seems no longer debatable.

At least three lines of interest and activity should be provided and carefully integrated in the total undertaking to this end: (1) there should be more tests and examinations; (2) there should be more student counseling and guidance; and (3) there should be more teacher training. (We do a poor job in the universities in training teachers for college and university work.)

These three activities should be bound together in such a way as to fortify the entire educational program of the institution. In time they should yield dependable appraisals of teaching performance. Then teachers of outstanding ability will have a chance to gain the prompt recognition to which they are entitled. When that time comes, and not before, teaching and research will become in fact, as they are now in doctrine, really co-ordinate functions of the American university.

Social Responsibilities of

Business Education

You will not be surprised to learn that some of my senti-
ments on this occasion [1] are of a paternal nature. I was in
on the conception of the Michigan School of Business Administration. I attended its birth. I cared for it, with able
assistants, in its infancy. I left it when it was still a youngster.
From a distance I have watched it grow in strength and
stature. I return after these twenty-odd years to find it in
young manhood already distinguished by recognized achievement, exceptional vitality, and outstanding promise. I find
it now in a wonderful new home of its own; its student enrollment over 1,200; its total graduates over 2,700. I would
not be human if I did not have some of the feelings of the
proud parent.

It was in February 1923 that I came to the University as
chairman of the Economics Department in the College of
Literature, Science, and the Arts. One of the understandings
with which I accepted this appointment was that I should
undertake a reorganization of the somewhat diverse cur-

[1] This was the twenty-fifth anniversary of the establishment of the
School of Business Administration, University of Michigan, October 5, 1949, at which Dr. Day delivered the convocation address.

107

ricula then being offered by the department. Some of these curricula were in business administration. Courses in the field of business administration had been given by the department as far back as the academic year 1889–90. A special certificate, awarded on graduation to those students who successfully completed certain course sequences in business administration, was introduced in 1914. But the status of instruction in business administration in 1923 was like that in sociology; both afforded undergraduate majors in the College of Literature, Science, and the Arts through course offerings of the Department of Economics.

It was in December 1923 that my report on the reorganization of the Economics Department went to President Burton and the Board of Regents. By far the most important single recommendation in the report was that a separate School of Business Administration be established and given complete responsibility for further activities of the University in this increasingly important field. This proposal was formally approved and adopted by the Board of Regents at a meeting on December 20, 1923. The School of Business Administration was established as of the beginning of the next fiscal year, that is, as of July 1, 1924.

As first Dean of the School, it was my privilege to direct the initiation of the new enterprise. I now have only general recollections of what my part in this was like. I do remember that the experience was a somewhat hectic one, especially as it had to do with the recruitment of the necessary staff. The School opened in September 1924, with a faculty of three professors, one associate professor, four assistant professors, two lecturers, and four instructors, and an entering class of twenty-two. We produced our first graduates—eleven of them —in June 1926. Interestingly enough, two of that first graduating class are members of the School's present roster of nineteen full professors.

The development of collegiate education for business over the past half-century makes a fascinating story. The academic status of business education fifty years ago was still somewhat dubious; its standing in business circles, relatively low. All that is now radically changed. In the quarter-century since this School was opened, collegiate business education has come of age. It has made a highly significant place for itself in both business and education. For this very reason it has become more than ever important that collegiate business education get a clear conception of its over-all responsibilities.

It is a mistake to think that business education is a kind of degraded general education, made available to those students who have neither the interest nor the ability to take general education of the traditional liberal arts type. The student in a collegiate school of business has to be given possession of certain specific basic skills. On graduation he should, for example, be in command of the techniques of quantitative analysis as these are applicable to the problems of business administration. He should have made at least a beginning in the successful cultivation of the kind of judgment that has to be brought to bear in the solution of business problems. If collegiate business schools do not turn out graduates who have a head start in the specific competences required in the manning of successful business enterprise, than these schools have no real reason for existence in the system of American higher education.

Some of the work of the collegiate schools of business may properly take the form of technical training. When a school offers an extensive series of courses in accounting and makes

109

it possible for some of its students to get the sort of training in this field that enables them in turn to qualify as certified public accountants, the school is not abandoning its role, provided these students at the same time get an understanding of the broad principles of business administration. The same goes for a number of other fields of technical specialization—in fact for any field in which the body of specialized, technical business knowledge is large enough to justify a sequence of courses of rigorous instructional content.

But contributions of basic skills and technical attainments alone will not give collegiate schools of business the stature they must acquire. In due course these schools should take their position among the great professional schools which constitute a distinguishing feature of American higher education.

The American university has achieved its present greatness in no small measure because of the place it has given to the professional school. It was not until the schools of law and medicine were drawn into the matrix of the university that their continued growth and development were assured. In the American university of today there is an interaction of professional and general education which is of profound significance for both. It is to this interaction that I wish to call your attention, particularly as it relates to the responsibilities of professional education for business.

The expression "professional education" is presumably the same in meaning as education for a profession. All sorts of occupations make claim to professional status. Few actually qualify. A profession is to be identified in terms of the following considerations:

1. Qualifying for the practice of a profession requires an extended course of specific training, this course entailing

substantial pre professional as well as professional studies.

2. The art practiced in a profession is subject to constant improvement through the contributions of wide-ranging scholarly and scientific research.

3. Obligations beyond those relating to the maintenance of current standards of professional practice are recognized, obligations relating to the public's need of better and possibly broader service.

Business administration does not yet fully conform to the specifications of the great learned professions. Perhaps it never will. For the art essential to success in business is not susceptible to the sort of close definition characteristic of practice in such professions as medicine, law, and engineering. It follows that the development of truly professional education for business may never be fully achieved. The fact remains that the aims of business education should be pointed in the professional direction. It is the public or social responsibilities of business administration *as a profession* that I have in mind when I say this.

Here I would call your attention to the stated aims of this Michigan School. These were originally stated, in the Preliminary Announcement issued in March 1924, six months before the School opened, as follows:

1. To provide instruction of professional grade in the basic principles of management.

2. To afford training in the use of quantitative measurement in the solution of management problems.

3. To assure education in the relationships between business leadership and the more general interests of the community.

Recently Dean Stevenson, in an article appearing in the July 1949 issue of the *Michigan Business Review,* has de-

111

scribed the scope of the School's instructional program in the following terms:

1. The basic and universal aspects of business.

2. The analysis of business problems.

3. Specialized and technical subjects in certain branches of business.

4. The position of businessmen in the social order and their relationship to the general welfare.

There are interesting differences of wording in these two statements, and there is greater emphasis on the specialized and technical in Dean Stevenson's, but at bottom the two are essentially to the same effect. In a conspicuous fashion both stress the importance of giving to business leadership through professional education a more definite sense of its public obligations.

As I see it, the indispensable contributions of business leadership in the generations ahead are related particularly to three vital social requirements. These I would identify as:

1. The achievement of a more constructive relationship between management and organized labor in the maintenance of profitable American commerce and industry.

2. The establishment of a more effective partnership between business and government in the necessary public regulation of private competitive enterprise.

3. The development of a greater public understanding of the essentials of the private enterprise system in the sound evolution of our national economy.

The number one problem of contemporary American economic life has to do with industrial and labor relations. In terms of national policy, we have committed ourselves to free labor organization and collective bargaining. Other types of arrangement and procedure still prevail in many quarters, but the general pattern is now firmly set. It will be through collective bargaining that the conditions of employment will be determined for the vast majority of industrial workers in this country—at least as long as the economy remains dominantly one of private enterprise.

During recent years labor organizations have grown enormously in strength. They have come to match in scope and power the paralleling organizations on the side of management. In some instances they have gone beyond this and now exert industry-wide controls. In some instances their powers are well-nigh monopolistic. Negotiation of the labor contract has become truly a battle of giants, in which much that goes on is a sheer testing of relative strength. Where the public interest comes in is at times hard to see.

The situation as it stands is unstable and unsatisfactory. We cannot rely upon the police power to settle industrial disputes if the numbers involved get too large and the emotional charge gets too high. How do you get the railroads to run if the railroadmen will not work? How do you get coal mined if the miners will not go into the pits? Forced labor has no place in a democracy; and there are real limits to the effective intervention of the state in attempts to resolve industrial disputes.

What is desperately needed is a broader base of common knowledge and mutual understanding in the continuous relationships of management and organized labor. This broader base is not likely to be quickly built. Deep prejudices still have to be eradicated. New philosophies have to be developed. New leaders have to take over in various quarters. But these are matters of goals, time, and effort. The professional schools of business have a great contribution to make in effecting the necessary changes.

113

The role of government in the supervision of the national economy cannot fail to be increasingly important. This follows from the nature of fundamental changes that have occurred over the years since the Republic was founded. Time was when the market was a place in which a substantial number of wholly independent sellers and buyers met to determine through bargaining the price at which the buyers could be induced to take all or practically all the goods or services the sellers had to offer. The essential conditions in such a market place were that both buyers and sellers were relatively numerous and acted independently.

These conditions no longer prevail over much of our industrial economy. Consolidation and concentration have been going on for so long that in some markets you can count on the fingers of one hand the number of sellers who are effectively competing. It follows that we cannot wisely depend as fully as we used to on the interaction of the forces of the market place. The old idea of "the less government, the better" no longer holds. The government now has important functions to perform in seeing that the public interest is suitably protected.

This is a function of government which cannot wisely be left to bureaucrats, even if they are operating at a high level of public authority. The experience and knowledge of business executives need to play into the formulations of government policy and the concrete administration of programs of regulation once these are adopted. What must be had is a working partnership of political and business leadership.

It is clear that we have not had the benefit of any such relationship between government and business in recent years. On the contrary, there has developed a general antipathy, which is now quite commonly taken for granted. This feel-

114

ing is due in part to a record of past abuses and excesses on the part of business, which gave rise to widespread public resentment. But the prevailing attitude toward big business is due in no small measure to manifest maneuver on the part of politicians seeking public support. Disparaging references to "Wall Street" and "economic royalists" have been expected to win votes. They have been used to that end. The public relations of business management have suffered in consequence, and thus far business management has failed, for a number of reasons, to put on a successful counter-offensive in its effort to regain public favor.

The fact remains that in times of crisis the politicians realize that they cannot successfully cope with the economic and financial problems of government without the assistance of the business leaders of the country. Witness what happened during World War II. Witness the employment of Paul Hoffman in the direction of the ECA program. It is unthinkable that the responsibilities of government in dealing with its vast range of problems affecting business enterprises in this country and abroad can be wisely discharged except as the wisdom of business leadership is utilized.

If this is to be accomplished, new attitudes must come to prevail in government and business quarters. A larger measure of mutual confidence and respect must be developed. All this calls for a basic reorientation on both sides. The professional schools of business administration have an important contribution to make in bringing about these necessary improvements.

Lurking behind the dissensions and conflicts which characterize our contemporary economic life is a growing threat to the essentials of our private competitive enterprise system. That system, in combination with the vast natural resources

115

of the North American continent, the energy and inventiveness of the American people, and the freedoms and protections provided by our governmental organization, has produced the highest standard of material well-being thus far achieved in the history of civilization. If collective experience is to be a guide, the essentials of this private competitive order should be retained. Meanwhile all over the world the drift is toward collectivism.

Resistance to this drift is not likely to be successfully developed in terms of the wisdom and vision of our leaders alone. Since the turn of the century, decisive power has come into the possession of the common man. We are now witnessing the combined effects of three great social developments: widening suffrage, popular education, and perfection of the techniques of modern mass communication. The net result of these developments has been a shift in the location of political power. It is the common man, asserting his newly acquired powers, who is most likely to determine the future of America in all its more important economic, political, and social phases.

If over the generations just ahead our private competitive enterprise system loses its vitality and ultimately its life, it will be because of public indifference and ignorance. The American people are not likely in any future now foreseeable to vote for the regimentations of the socialist state nor the brutalities of the Communist regime. What may happen is a subtle and continuous invasion of the blood stream of our economic system until it perishes from an incurable pernicious anemia.

The only means of preventing any such course of events is to give to the American people *as a whole* a thoroughgoing understanding of the essential elements of the private com-

116

petitive enterprise system. In achieving this end business leadership must join hands with educational and political leadership. No time is to be lost in bringing these combined forces to bear. The potential role of the schools of business in this undertaking is of the utmost importance.

Education in Industrial

and Labor Relations:

THE SCHOOL AT CORNELL UNIVERSITY

Labor's stake and interest in education are of long standing, and labor's contribution to education has been a notable one. The attitude of organized labor toward the American public school system has been clearly established for generations past. The beginnings of the labor movement in this country date back about a century and a quarter. At the very outset of this movement larger educational opportunity was insistently demanded. I quote from one of the most widely known authorities on the history of American labor, John R. Commons:

The first awakening of American wage earners as a class did not occur until the late twenties (1820). . . . The cause of the awakening was economic and political inequalities between citizens of different classes, not primarily between employers and wage earners but between producers and consumers. Around two chief grievances, both closely related to their status as citizens of a democracy, the working men of this period rallied. First was the demand for leisure which furnishes the keynote of the economic movement. . . . Second was the demand for the con-

118

sideration of public education which furnished the keynote of the political movement. Charity schools were held to be incompatible with citizenship, for they degraded the workmen and failed to furnish them with the requisite training and information for consideration of public questions, thereby dooming them to become dupes of political demagogues. . . . In 1829, public education took its place distinctly and definitely at the head of the list of measures urged by the Working Men's Party. . . . And the candidates for the State Legislature nominated by the Working Men's Party were pledged to favor a general system of state education.

This early stand of labor on the subject of public education has been consistently maintained ever since. True, labor has at times been critical of what the schools have had to offer. It has frequently contended that the schools were not adequately serving the interests of the working class, especially on the side of vocational training. But generally speaking, labor has strongly backed the idea of increasing the provision of popular education through the American public school system.

On the side of higher education, the attitude of organized labor, generally speaking, has not been so clear. This is doubtless due in part to the fact that what goes on in higher education has not seemed to labor to bear directly on the interests and needs of the working class. But another explanation has been the distrust which labor has felt toward the prevailing controls of higher education, especially in the private institutions. Labor as such has had little or no voice in the direction of the affairs of our colleges and universities, hence the conclusion of labor that these institutions could not be depended upon to serve the interests of labor. The result has been the establishment of educational enterprises

119

under the direct and sole control of labor. This development has challenged the very idea of higher education as an inclusive public service. It has moreover constituted a reversal of the position taken by labor a hundred years ago at the time of the establishment of the so-called land-grant colleges —of which Cornell University is one. Then the working class joined with the farmers in demanding the creation in each state of a people's college. The need for such institutions is just as clear today as it was then. Fortunately we are well on the way to getting them.

The establishment of the New York State School of Industrial and Labor Relations is concrete evidence of this fact. This new educational enterprise was not the result of planning by educators. It was at the outset the brain child of a committee of the State Legislature—the Joint Legislative Committee on Industrial and Labor Conditions. Under the distinguished chairmanship of the Honorable Irving M. Ives this committee had done notable work ever since 1938 in the improvement of industrial and labor conditions throughout the state. It had worked for better laws, for more effective administration of the state agencies operating in this field, for greater understanding all around of the issues involved in industrial controversy. Out of its experience and deliberations, the Joint Committee came to certain basic conclusions. Perhaps the most basic of all was best expressed in the following statement in the Committee's 1940 Report to the Governor and Legislature:

The most satisfactory and happiest human relationships are the product not of legal compulsion, but rather of voluntary determination among human beings to cooperate with one another. Though we may legislate to the end of time, there will never be industrial peace and harmony without good faith, integrity, a high degree of responsibility, and a real desire to cooperate on the part of all parties concerned. Without this spirit of good will, all of the social, economic and labor laws of man will prove eventually to be in vain.

This fundamental conclusion led the Committee to turn more and more of its attention to the bearing of education on industrial and labor relations. Extensive surveys were made of existing efforts to educate in this field. Out of these studies certain conclusions were drawn. I quote from the 1942 Report:

The Committee believes that New York State must lead the way in providing training in this field. There is no adequate substitute which can be of greater potential value in promoting sound and peaceful industrial and labor relations. Only as the representatives of employers and workers are equipped to discuss the problems of industrial organization and labor stabilization with equivalent technical information and competence, can we hope to maintain and advance the economic welfare of the state.

The Committee in 1942 recommended that a School of Industrial and Labor Relations be established at Cornell University. It was not until two years later that formal action was taken on this proposal. Then by action of the Legislature, with subsequent approval of Governor Dewey—who has backed the project wholeheartedly from the very beginning—the New York State School was created. A Temporary Board of Trustees was constituted to develop plans for the School more completely.

The recommendations of the Temporary Board went to the Governor and Legislature of the state on February 19, 1945. Perhaps the most important single recommendation had to do with the control of the School. Here the proposal

121

was that the School be placed under the Board of Trustees of Cornell University, subject to the condition that the Cornell charter be amended to provide that the University's Board be enlarged to include three members elected by the Board from the field of New York state labor, and the Industrial Commissioner, and the Commissioner of Commerce of the State of New York, both serving as members ex officio. These conditions were accepted by the Cornell Board of Trustees. The Legislature and Governor acted favorably, in the following April, on the Temporary Board's recommendations, and as of July 1, 1945, the New York State School of Industrial and Labor Relations became a going educational enterprise. An advisory council for the School was immediately created by action of the Cornell Trustees. This council includes representatives of labor, management, government, education, and the University.

Mr. Ives was made the first Dean. Soon thereafter he went to Washington as United States Senator from New York. In the summer of 1947 the School was placed under the sustained direction of an experienced administrative head in the person of the former and first New York State Commissioner of Commerce, Martin P. Catherwood.

Those first few months of the new School were hectic, indeed. We had to get an administrative staff. We had to recruit a new faculty from top to bottom. We had to select a student body. We had to organize a program of instruction. We had to find improvised quarters in other University buildings. Most important of all, we had to explain ourselves, for in certain quarters there were doubts about the wisdom of our undertaking. As I look back on those days, I wonder that we made out as well as we did. We certainly could not

122

have done so if the capacity of the guiding personnel and the morale of the entire group had not been high.

Since that time a lot of progress has been made. The state has been generous in supplying necessary funds. Temporary quarters for the School have been erected. The program of resident professional instruction is now in full swing. The first batch of graduates has been produced. Extension courses are now being offered in the principal industrial centers of the state. Important research work is going forward. Informational services and significant publications have been launched. Despite the fact that the undertaking has had to break new ground in every direction, it is now thoroughly established and making a reputation for itself far and wide.

The fact remains that the School still faces certain fundamental problems. Thus, we still have to win fuller understanding of what it is the School is endeavoring to do. There are still those who think we are trying to produce more astute labor agitators. Nothing could be further from the truth. In a word, the aim of the School is to improve industrial and labor relations. This the School proposes to do by organizing and offering the means of more knowledge and better understanding among those in organized labor, management, and government who are likely to determine the course of industrial and labor relations in this country.

It was Samuel Gompers who once said: "Whatever progress the American labor movement makes rests on an educational basis." It was a businessman who recently said: "We need to do a gigantic job of air-conditioning in labor relations. We need to sweep from our minds the cobwebs of ignorance. For we cannot get mutual understanding with-

123

out mutual knowledge. We cannot get mutual knowledge without mutual education."

It is this ideal of mutual education which lies at the heart of this unique and exciting educational adventure in the New York State School. The Joint Legislative Committee, which originally conceived the School, stressed this idea. I quote from the Committee's 1943 Report:

The Committee believes [however] that a state-sponsored school in this state should be based upon a broader educational philosophy. One of the most important ways of improving industrial and labor relations is to bring together, in a common training program, representatives of both labor and industry. What is important here is not merely attendance at the same institution or in the same school but rather mutual and cooperative analysis of the problems common to both groups.

The leading idea in the New York State School is that of putting students through a program of instruction, information, discussion, research, and experience which is substantially identical, whether subsequently they find themselves in the service of labor organizations, of management, or of government. Later graduates of the School are likely to find themselves on opposite sides of the same table. We hope they will. We expect they will. If and when that time comes, and they are in responsible relationship to the contending parties, we expect something is going to happen to the nature of the negotiations. Not that all issues will be resolved; there will doubtless still be conflicting concerns and interests; but we confidently expect that at times there will be a larger measure of common understanding, common appreciation, common knowledge of what is involved in the pending issues. That is the goal of our program, and it is toward that goal that we are moving.

124

A second major problem with which the new School is confronted is the satisfactory placement of its graduates. They are not failing of employment. By and large they are getting good jobs. But the opportunities for them in organized labor are severely limited. It will doubtless be some time before the labor organizations of the country come to see the importance of expert staff in the fields covered by the School's professional offering. Until that time the services of the School which are most likely to interest labor directly are those made available through extension, information, and research. Ultimately, it is to be hoped, organized labor will see the advantage to itself of the professionally trained men and women the School will be producing. And it will be helpful to labor, of course, as these graduates show up in key positions in management and government; certainly it will if the School succeeds in imparting the larger measure of knowledge and understanding which is its aim.

The most critically important problems in the School of Industrial and Labor Relations over the years are almost certain to relate to the role of education in democracy's handling of its own internal conflicts. We live in a time of dissension and conflict. Much of what goes on currently represents little more than a testing of relative strength by contending forces of great proved or potential power. We all recognize this readily in the international sphere. It is in fact almost equally evident in domestic affairs.

Phenomenal changes have taken place in American commerce and industry since the turn of the century. The most striking changes have had to do with the size of the dominant competing organizations. Business consolidations have created huge and powerful units in their respective fields; similarly labor organizations have brought vast areas of opera-

125

tion within the reach of their interest and control. The early American enterprise system developed in quite a different national economy. It long since demonstrated its extraordinary productiveness. In combination with the amazing natural resources of the North American continent and the unmatched initiative and energy of the American people, this economy has brought a standard of living for the mass of the people the like of which the world has never seen. But this economy now has to adapt itself to new conditions, the most significant of which is the greatly increased scale of the dominant competing units. It would seem to be clear that the essentials of private competitive enterprise privately financed must be preserved. We are not likely to come out with this end result, however, unless the contending parties learn how to co-operate as well as compete.

This necessary co-operation must recognize the fact that profits and wages come out of the same pot, and that unless both are in the contents in adequate measure, the pot will not long supply either profits or wages. In short, both wages and profits depend upon the ability and willingness of labor and management to create conditions under which private competitive enterprise can prosper.

Organized labor of late years has come into possession of unprecedented power. In some quarters this power is being abused. The consequent challenge to our free institutions is perfectly apparent. As was recently remarked in the columns of *The Reporter:*

There is a point in the legal system of every democratic nation at which conflicts that affect too large a number of people or involve interests of too great magnitude cannot be settled by the rule of law, even if the law is supported by police power unless,

126

of course, the police power prevails and democracy is given up.

It follows that the powers possessed by labor can work to the advantage of the American people only if they are exercised with a wise and sustained sense of public responsibility. It is here that wider knowledge and deeper understanding are indispensable. It is toward the acquisition and dissemination of such knowledge and understanding that the New York State School is resolved to work with all the resources at its command. The course the School has charted looks toward truly democratic relationships among labor, management, and government, with each recognizing and respecting the authorities and the responsibilities of the other. Such relationships are our last hope. With them we can achieve peace with prosperity. Without them free America will be lost.

It has become commonplace to say that contemporary civilization is in crisis. It is. The advantages of freedom, which we have so long taken for granted, are being sharply challenged; not only that, they are being formidably attacked; in some quarters they are yielding ground. Certain lessons we must learn. We can, if necessary, in a great emergency, *protect* democracy for the time being with military might or with the police power. We can never *produce* democracy by any such means. Democracy as a way of living together in peace, as a means of achieving justice and prosperity, lives in the hearts and minds of men and women of courage and conscience. It can get its continuing sustenance nowhere else.

It follows inescapably that in the long run we must look

to the church and the home and the school to fortify our democratic ways. That certainly goes for the great areas of conflict and controversy, of which, for the moment at least, the most significant in American life is the field of industrial and labor relations. Hence, the significance of this challenging pioneering effort that is going forward in the New York State School of Industrial and Labor Relations.

Role of Administration
in Higher Education

PERHAPS a pathological note will serve to introduce the subject. One of the most widely prevalent disorders of academic life in America is an antipathy toward administrative officers on the part of professional staff. This disorder is not related to any particular type of organic structure; it is essentially a manifestation of functional disturbance. A certain amount of such disturbance may be considered normal, like an occasional attack of indigestion. It may reflect nothing more than a mild resentment of the power which administration is bound to exercise. But, when the symptoms become either pronounced or acute, the disorder is serious business; for, as with other psychosomatic manifestations, like ulcers of the stomach, the persistence of the symptoms suggests some deep-seated and sustained internal tension. Factors of distrust, suspicion, and fear are almost certain to be present. The cumulative effect of tensions of this sort may be to put the sufferer completely out of commission. This happens to institutions just as it does to individuals.

Of course there are situations in which tensions of this sort are so highly personalized that only operative procedures can be successful. The offending members, be they admin-

129

istrative or professional, have to be excised, or at least insulated. But much more frequently the tensions arise not from personalities but from failure to observe sound rules of associated action, or from ignorance or misunderstanding of the functions of administration in academic organization. It is here that there are opportunities for sound therapeutic measures. A wider appreciation of the role of administration in our colleges and universities should help materially in reducing the disorder which we now find so widely prevalent. Hence I am led to undertake this brief enumeration of the contributions that sound administration may be expected to make in a complex academic organization such as a great university.

In discussions of this important subject it is customary to note that the functions of administration in academic life are secondary in the sense that the teaching and research for which colleges and universities exist can be carried on only by the professional staff. From this point of view, administration justifies itself only as it facilitates and strengthens the work of the teachers and scholars. At bottom this is true enough, and certainly we can all admit that administration is never an end in itself but only a means to an end. Nevertheless, it can be an indispensable means. It is important for all concerned that we see clearly what administration has to contribute, what in fact must be assigned to administration if the over-all purposes of academic institutions are to be realized. Let us consider briefly what some of these major responsibilities of administration are.

The most obvious and best recognized obligation of administration is to add to the institution's resources. The task of obtaining additional funds is in fact so characteristic of the role of the college and university president that he is frequently described as more of a cultured mendicant than anything else. It is safe to say that the reputation of many presidents has derived largely from their success or failure as fund-raisers.

The explanation of this is relatively simple. Here is one type of accomplishment which is almost certain to provoke general acclaim. With new funds, the president can implement new undertakings and gain fresh support for his overall program. A million dollars of new money can quiet a lot of carping criticism of any administration. It is altogether natural that any college or university administration should turn its attention increasingly to the problem of finding additional support for the work of the institution, since the administration's ability to give effect to its own constructive planning may depend largely upon the possibility of finding new financial resources. In short, there is no line of administrative activity as safe as that of the vigorous solicitation of new money, whether such money comes from private or public sources. Few will complain if an administration so occupies itself, providing it does so successfully.

There is, however, a danger in administrative absorption in this type of activity; for, in efforts to obtain additional funds, important concessions may need to be made with respect to the fundamental purposes of the institution. Moreover, serious distortions may come into the allocation of the administration's total energy and drive. There is, in my opinion, a definite connection between the lack of adequate educational leadership in American academic life today and the common involvement of administration in all-out fund-raising activities.

Another major responsibility of academic administration has to do with the institution's public relations. The president

131

is chief custodian of the reputation and prestige of the institution he heads. This means that he must be constantly concerned with the public's reception of the institution's activities. Professors and students alike have their ways of complicating these public relationships. Of course it is not difficult to make the work of many scholars and scientists contribute directly and substantially to the prestige of the institution's work. But professors enjoy an extraordinary independence, which they do not hesitate to exercise on a wide variety of occasions. The late Carl Becker, distinguished historian and a great defender of academic freedom, was fond of saying that "a professor is a man who thinks otherwise." Professors certainly are likely to do just that, not only in their own fields of specialization, but also in areas which lie outside their special competence. It is no mean task to keep the professor appropriately explained to the public. College students similarly can embarrass the public relations of the institutions they attend. It can be said in general that college students get a bad press. Their serious undertakings get little attention; their foibles and frivolities make news. It is no small part of the responsibility of administration in American academic life to give the public an understanding of what the professors and students are really doing, and the very high values that lie in the program of education and research in which they are engaged. The public relations of our colleges and universities need much more attention than they have had. This is a responsibility which lodges clearly in the hands of administration.

A third important assignment of administration has to do with the task of mediation within the institution. A college or university is made up of many disparate elements: trustees, faculty, administrative staff, students, alumni. It is divulging no secret to say that professors frequently need to be interpreted to trustees, and trustees to professors. The importance of the teacher needs to be explained to the man largely engaged in research, and vice versa. The scientists and humanists do not always understand one another. The same is sometimes true of faculty and students. There is thus a widespread need of effecting a larger measure of understanding and appreciation among these different groups, and headway along these lines is not likely to be made except as administration exerts positive leadership.

This work of internal mediation looks toward another important responsibility of administration; namely, the effective co-ordination of the wide variety of interests and activities which constitute the total program of the institution. In many respects the different subdivisions of a great university are in competition with one another. By their very nature, the different subdivisions are made up of specialists who naturally see the work of the institution primarily in terms of their own particular undertakings. It is altogether appropriate that these specialists think somewhat obsessively about their own interests; they are not likely otherwise to exhibit the drive they should have. For this very reason they cannot be expected to be adept in compromise or reciprocal adjustment. It is a special function of administration, with its over-all view of all the parts, to see that all of the activities are appropriately manned and meshed so as to give maximum effectiveness to the total operation. This has the effect, of course, of throwing academic administration very considerably into the field of personnel management. One of the largest responsibilities of administration is to maintain morale throughout the organization, at the same time that the drives of various parts of the organization are kept under the restraints necessary if complete co-ordination is to be obtained.

Another inescapable obligation of administration is to provide for innovations. From time to time new departments have to be created, new schools and colleges constituted, major realignments or readjustments in existing departments or divisions initiated. Generally speaking, the impulses which lead to these innovations do not come from the professional staff. Quite naturally, the organization as it stands is likely to view with skepticism any major additions to program which may set up fresh competition for available funds. It is fair to say that by and large academic organization is resistant to change. The *status quo* tends to root itself deeply in academic soil. It is only as administration deals vigorously with new possibilities that wise additions to the undertakings of the institution, if and when opportunities offer, will be initiated.

Finally, it is the task of administration to identify and express the general philosophy for which the institution stands. It is not likely that any college or university will have achieved an outstanding position except as it has maintained a tradition and has kept faith with important ideals. But characteristically, neither tradition nor ideals have been clearly formulated. They tend to remain vague and inarticulate. Colleges and universities must recognize fundamental purposes. They must have a sense of order and direction. In these days of universal confusion it is of paramount importance that the institutions of higher learning make more clearly evident the fundamental purposes to which they propose to devote the resources of which they are possessed. It is not enough for them to stand simply for the spread of knowledge. They must stand for a definite moral and spiritual commitment. Nothing short of this will suffice. There is no responsibility of administration quite so important as that of rallying the forces of colleges and universities to a clear enunciation of fundamental social philosophy. The president, as head of the administration, must stand as the chief spokesman of this philosophy, once it has been clearly formulated.

I am sure I have said enough to make it clear that the contract assumed by the head of a great institution is one of huge proportions. Administration may be only a means to an end, but it is none the less of supreme importance. Alongside the responsibilities which administration cannot avoid must be a commensurate authority and power. This authority and power must provide for the exercise of necessary discrimination. If excellence is to be rewarded, many decisions cannot be left to balloting. Administration cannot possibly contribute what it must to academic life if it is viewed with distrust or suspicion, or if its powers are subjected to unwarranted checks and curbs.

If the analysis I have presented is accepted, it is clear enough that the qualities requisite in the academic administrator are, indeed, exacting. He must be a man of wise and farseeing vision, who can keep in mind the purposes for which the institution stands and the practical means of their attainment. He must be a man of unfailing fairness of judgment. He must be capable of magnanimity in the face of unwarranted criticism or opposition. He must establish a record of justice in all his dealings. He cannot possibly succeed if he is lacking in courage and fortitude. He must be willing to take chances and to take the consequences of his action. He will not last long if he fails to maintain an inner calm, serenity in the face of the stresses and strains of high office.

135

It is not surprising that the job of college or university president has been described from time to time as an impossible one. Certainly in many ways it makes demands which cannot be entirely fulfilled. Nevertheless, we have our truly great college and university presidents, men who, to an extraordinary degree, establish the kind of leadership their institutions need.

A University President Talks

About His Job

I HAVE often wondered what it feels like to be a pinch hitter in an important baseball game! It has always seemed to me that it might not be too bad, for usually a pinch hitter is a good hitter put in to hit for a pitcher who can't hit. Stepping in as a pinch hitter for Babe Ruth, however, would be something else; and I have some of the sensations of being thrown into this particular kind of assignment without the qualifications for filling it. But when I heard of the predicament of my faculty associates in charge of this project as they learned that the scheduled speaker could not get here, I decided that I would exercise the normal function of my office and talk!

Although what I have to say is not carefully prepared—there hasn't been any time for that—I can assure you that it is not "off the cuff," for it stems from some real and poignant experiences in the work of this great institution.

Almost exactly a year ago, I had a letter from a member of the Board of Trustees of Cornell, a copy of which went simultaneously to all other members of the board. When I receive any letter, copies of which go to numerous other persons, I suspect that its purpose is not entirely evident on its face. I was confident that this was true of this particular

137

communication which came from one of the most distinguished and able industrialists in the country, a man who is
a leader not only in industrial affairs but also in important
governmental advisory services. The letter made a very
strong plea for the introduction of a required course at
Cornell on the American Way of Life. It went on to point
out that democracy is in jeopardy and that we should bring
to bear all available resources in its defense. It further asserted that the colleges and universities of the country have
a very important role to play in this undertaking and that
certainly Cornell, with its great tradition of freedom and responsibility, should make its own unique contribution: hence
this formal proposal that there be a compulsory course in the
American Way of Life, required of every degree candidate
on this campus before he is certified as a Cornell graduate.

In some ways, that communication struck a responsive
note. I have long been deeply interested in the problem of
how to safeguard our democratic tradition in America, and
I have long thought that education was certain to be the
ultimate line of defense. Ten years ago I offered these observations in dealing with the general subject of what threatens American democracy:

The democracies will, if they can, deal effectively with the most
serious of all threats to democracy—the indifference, complacency and ignorance of those who have shared democracy's
benefits. We Americans simply take democracy for granted. We
have no awareness of what we would suffer if our democratic
privileges were removed. We fail to sense what espionage, terror-
ism, completely arbitrary and despotic rule would mean to us
individually. We make no sustained effort to understand what
democracy is. We are prone to think of it as a system of government, rather than a form of human relationship in which men

and women of every class and creed live together in peace. We fail to practice democracy in our daily living. We show no determination to make our individual contributions that democracy may be preserved and strengthened. We exhibit no lasting devotion to the common ideal. From *these* deficiencies come the really serious threats to American democracy.

Having said that ten years ago, and on even earlier occasions, I was prepared to give earnest consideration to this proposal coming from a member of the Board of Trustees. For certainly we face the problem among the American people of acquiring an adequate interest in democracy; even more, of gaining a deep understanding of what democracy really is; and last, but not least, of developing a sufficient devotion to our American democratic ideals.

But as President of Cornell I had to take a somewhat evasive position with respect to this communication. I had to say that under the by-laws of this institution its educational program is in the custody of the University faculty. Hence I took a noncommittal position and said I would promptly relay the proposal to the appropriate faculty authorities, which I did.

That immediately raised some very interesting questions of internal management and leadership. Fortunately, the authorities of the University faculty approved the proposal, except for certain of its terms. Quite naturally, and I would say reasonably, the faculty rejected almost at once the idea that there should be a *compulsory* course, which, generally speaking, is alien to the Cornell tradition and probably impracticable anyway. Cornell students have a way of being negatively suggestible to any compulsions the faculty may undertake to impose. I would venture the opinion that the way to kill this course at the outset would be to make it

139

required; and that the way to build up its prestige would be to make it a strictly voluntary affair.

The compulsion that lies in a professional course, like medicine or engineering, is quite different from the compulsion you have in a course like Freshman English. Any student who has committed himself to the acquisition of professional competence will ordinarily follow the advice of the faculty in what he must learn in order to become qualified to practice. Therefore, the psychology of a required course in engineering or in law or in medicine is somewhat different.

Perhaps the requirement of Freshman English is more analogous, and I'm tempted to rest my case on what you observe in that course. That is an example in which compulsion exhibits all its frailties. I'd hate to reproduce it in something even more important; namely, the cultivation of an understanding and appreciation of our democratic ideals. We may be able to build up a sentiment on the basis of which we can require of all our degree candidates an understanding of these American ideals, but I should not like to commit the program to that kind of handicap until it had proven itself on a voluntary, experimental basis. I should hope that we could build up a content, either in the course or its accessories, which would attract a great deal of student attention, and possibly in time develop a tradition in favor of all students taking these units of instruction. But I would definitely be opposed to making the course compulsory at the outset. Imagine the problem to staff such a course required of a couple of thousand students and to get real value out of every exploration of some of the vast complexities of this subject of American democracy.

140

Of course, I would hope that, sooner or later, all young people would be effectively exposed to a course of this type. But, as I have said on other occasions, the task of transmitting to American youth an understanding, appreciation, and devotion to the democratic tradition really belongs in the secondary schools, where required units can be easily injected into the program. As a matter of fact, it is here that young people are likely to be much more impressionable than they are at the level of college. So, as matters stand now, I would reject promptly the idea of making this a course required of all Cornell degree candidates. We might try it out on the Arts college; I'd hesitate a long while to try it out on the engineers!

There was a very important challenge about this proposal from the Cornell trustee, for the colleges and universities of the country have not been sufficiently alerted to their responsibilities in giving the American people an understanding of democracy. Our great fundamental democratic documents date from a period more than 150 years ago in which this country represented a very different type of society. We were then a rural, agricultural people, governed very largely through the suffrage of freeholders. There were no great cities; there were no great centers of industry, with masses of people dependent on employers for their livelihood, and without property or other means of maintaining themselves when off the job. Certainly, anybody who thinks of the America of 1950 and contrasts it with the America of 1787 is bound to marvel that any constitutional system created under those earlier conditions could have survived as well as ours has. There is, however, a vast task of reinterpretation and reformulation to be done in gaining a full

141

understanding of what democracy means in a highly urban and highly industrialized modern society and in a world of atomic power.

The proposal that we organize formal instruction on this subject of the American Way of Life or American Democracy presented a definite challenge. Hence, I learned with great interest and satisfaction of the creation by the University faculty of an able committee to develop this project into a concrete educational program. I have great hopes for it. We have included in our first appeal for additional funds in support of a Greater Cornell an item of $500,000 with which we propose to endow a permanent chair in American Values, and attach to that chair a variety of related services, designed to focus the attention of this University community on the importance of gaining a fresh understanding of American tradition and ideals. As a member of both the University faculty and the University administration, I am prepared to announce publicly that I shall bring all the powers at my disposal to the support of this undertaking. I want to see Cornell step out front in a sharp, dramatic formulation of the American democratic ideal.

The problems of administration here at Cornell in defending American democracy relate to a lot of things besides curriculum revision. I would like to see all parts of this University contribute to these curricular undertakings; but I would like also to see all parts of this great University contribute to the development of sounder relationships between administration and our distinguished company of scholars and scientists who constitute the essential part of a great university.

As I contemplate the administration-faculty relationship, I am impressed with what I should call certain deficiencies in the present situation. In the first place, I think some misunderstanding exists with respect to the role of administration. Administration is accessory in any college or university. It is constituted to facilitate the essential functions of teaching and research. As the administration undertakes to do this, however, it must assume certain responsibilities which to some extent invade the premises of the scholars and scientists. The university administration, along with trustees, is bound to have the last word in determining the placement of available resources. It has also the critically important job of undertaking some sort of appraisal of those who constitute the company of scholars and scientists. There is no way to dispose of that very trying problem except as administration deals with it, wisely and fairly. I would like, however, to see the professors share with administration the job of evaluation. This is the most important single responsibility of administration, and it is one that should be shared, in some measure at least, by the scholars and scientists themselves.

In final analysis, all parts of this institution are equally affected by the relative efficiency or inefficiency of the total operation. If the operation is inefficient, all contribute to the cost. We need a freer communication of ideas, proposals, and judgments between the administration and faculty. There must be mutual respect and confidence. Furthermore, there is no chance whatever of advancing the over-all aims of a great university save as there exists throughout the entire organization a sense of common purpose. That is not easy to effect in a large body of able and distinguished specialists. Quite naturally, most of them are primarily concerned with their own particular fields of activity. They are humanists or nuclear physicists, lawyers or doctors, and, as such, if

143

they are good, they are very largely engrossed in their particular interests. The great problem of university administration is to get some sense of common purpose in the entire company, some feeling of attachment to a single corporate enterprise.

Suppose we next consider administration-alumni relationships. Nobody can imagine the extraordinary diversity of the complaints of the alumni. If it isn't one thing, it's another. I travel occasionally, so I encounter these complaints in the flesh. I don't believe anybody can surprise me with one I haven't heard before, although last week one came to me which I hadn't heard for some time. One alumnus of the institution declared he would never give anything more to the University because we put Olin Hall where we did— right in the middle of the Sage College slope!

The complaint of the proud and fond parent whose child doesn't make the grade is the most common of all. I had a prize one of that kind just two days ago. An alumnus was saying he just couldn't understand how such things happened. He's seen it happen with his own son, and now it happened with the son of one of his friends. Knowing some of the Cornell students who were actually on campus, he could not imagine how these two deserving boys had been rejected. I made it a point to look at the records of these boys. The alumnus' son stood 498 in a class of 523! On the occasion on which he was interviewed the charm of his personality was recorded. But somehow, personality doesn't fare too well with the faculty on this campus unless it is accompanied by a measure of intellectual power.

Those complaints are hard to take—and they involve a considerable amount of alienation. We get more serious complaints about some of our educational undertakings. For a

144

period of about two years I was hammered from both sides on the "terrible blunder" Cornell had made in accepting the New York State School of Industrial and Labor Relations. Apparently that school was to be one of two totally incompatible things: a school for labor agitators, or a school in which labor's leadership was broken down under the malign influence of management!

It is a formidable task to work out the administration-alumni relationship without sacrificing some aspects of reason, without yielding on the general principle of equality of opportunity, and without selling downstream the concept and ideal of democracy in America. Some graduates seem to regard Cornell as an exclusive club. It is, of course, a very fine club. That's why they want their children in it. But the idea that admission is strictly on merit, and that this institution from its outset has opened wide its doors to the young of every class, creed, color, and race apparently does not register in many quarters.

However, while these complaints sometimes seem to loom large as I travel and meet with Cornellians, I am tremendously impressed with their loyalty and devotion to the University. They may not discern clearly some aspects of the great significance of Cornell, but they'll go along with Cornell through thick and thin just the same. So, as I see it, the problem of administration in this particular area is to build on this splendid sentiment, affection, gratitude, and devotion, concepts of equality and democracy in harmony with the great purpose of Cornell.

Finally, let us consider administration-student relationships. These appear to have come somewhat to the fore these days, thanks to a student paper which momentarily displays a great deal of zest. The tradition of this campus is supposed to be a combination of freedom and responsibility. A good deal of the time the freedom appears most in evidence. I'm for both. I delight in the fact that the students on this campus largely are on their own. The community they have created tends to be democratic; its aspirations are certainly democratic; and its government is by such free election as we can manage. But community life on the campus suffers from certain weaknesses, the most inescapable of which is that the constituency is constantly shifting. Imagine what it would be like to run any city or town, county or state if the entire population moved out every four years and an entirely new population moved in. Well, that's what happens in this little democratic community. Leadership becomes pretty well established and, by the end of the senior year, seems to be exhibiting a gratifying amount of understanding and wisdom. Then it is tapped at graduation exercises, and it goes! A new crop then comes up, and we start all over again.

I am delighted to see more student activity in the affairs of the Cornell campus. That, to my way of thinking, begins to spell democracy. But I am a bit concerned about some things. One is an apparent unwillingness on the part of some students to get all the facts relevant to issues with which they concern themselves. This is exacting a great deal, for many of these problems are not simple. They involve a tremendous amount of background, and they have had a great deal of attention from faculty, administration, or trustees. If the students wish to participate in the administration of this institution, I would suggest that they reduce their programs of formal study to a part-time schedule and devote the remainder of their time to some of these problems. Short of that, I think that it is inevitable that a good many opinions circulate which are not adequately supported by complete knowledge of the factors involved. Unless there is a responsible relationship in the solution of these problems, many of which are pressing and impinge quite naturally on the interests of the students, I am sure we are almost certain to move into a kind of chronic dissension and disunity. That is an affliction from which all democracy suffers, and which may in time prove to be its undoing.

In these days all sorts of minority pressure groups are trying to forward their own special interests. The majority doesn't get equally agitated about these issues because it lacks the same sort of special interest. The end result is a kind of contention, commotion, and agitation which keeps institutions and governmental agencies alike off balance. I am not suggesting that these things be suppressed. I welcome full discussion of every problem that exists in this institution and outside it. The more calm, dispassionate, well-informed discussion we can have of these matters, the better off we will all be. I'm for discussion; I'm for student activities; I'm for student participation. But I want it to be deliberate and responsible, and that takes time, thought, and effort. Failing these, we're likely to have misunderstanding, if not acrimonious dispute, and thus render conditions acute which must not be allowed to become so.

So, with regard to student-administration relationships, as with faculty-administration relationships and alumni-administration relationships, I say: "Let's free the channels of communication; let's come at our problems with feelings of mutual respect and confidence; and let's keep uniformly in mind a sense of corporate enterprise and a sense of deepest devotion to the great ideals of human relationships which are essentials of American democracy."

147

This has become more than a thumbnail sketch of some of the problems with which administration at Cornell has to deal, and of the general attitude of administration. I have said on more than one occasion that I deem myself to be among those most rarely privileged in my time. Why? Because I have had a chance to serve an institution which seems to me to express more fully the ideals of American democracy to which I am profoundly attached than any other institution I know.

Utilization of Human

Resources in a Cold War:

The Conant Plan

As a people we Americans have had a single basic policy for utilizing human resources in our part of the world in time of peace. We have spelled this policy out in terms of individual freedom and responsibility, equality of opportunity, social mobility, fair competition, private enterprise, public provision of certain over-all services, but careful avoidance of governmental regimentation. While these are all ideals not yet fully attained, they are more nearly approximated in actual practice in the United States than in any other great nation in the world. Thanks to this type of utilization of *human* resources on a continent blessed with immense *natural* resources, we Americans have demonstrated a productiveness and established a living standard never equaled in all human history. Individual freedom and initiative as a way of utilizing human resources in time of peace has worked, and worked wonders.

We have not been so clear in our thinking about the utilization of human resources in time of war. We started out with the idea that even in war individual initiative in the form of voluntary service would meet national requirements. True, we set up certain special inducements to enlistments, the common one being a bonus in the form of a grant of public land. However, it was not until the Civil War had been fought for two years that we finally resorted to a draft. We are all familiar with the fact that this action of the Federal Government met with opposition and in certain localities gave rise to rioting. This happened despite the fact that under the Civil War draft one could hire a substitute if one had the money and could find the able-bodied taker. It was really not until World War I that the American people came to see clearly that in war, at least as war is now conducted, there is no substitute for compulsory service through the provisions of a National Service Act. We had the draft in World War I. We had Selective Service in World War II. Everyone now recognizes that, given war, the ideal of individual freedom and initiative has to be put aside and the principle of governmental compulsion put in its place. Volunteering in a time of great emergency will not do for at least two reasons: (1) it does not yield an adequate flow of personnel; and (2) it results in an unsound channeling of total manpower. Clearly enough, in time of war, the utilization of human resources must be explicitly and absolutely in the hands of the national authorities.

In view of this basic difference of policy in the utilization of human resources, on the one hand in time of peace, and on the other in time of war, we are faced crucially with the question: Under what conditions are we now operating? Are we living in a time of war or a time of peace?

When we consider our current undertakings in Korea, it certainly looks like war. But there has been no declaration of war, nor any official acknowledgment of a state of war. Technically we have joined the United Nations in an attempt to thwart armed aggression. Our announced intentions are not warlike; and could the United Nations have their way, the conflict in Korea would come quickly to an end.

On the other hand our relations with Soviet Russia since 1945 cannot be described accurately as peaceful. We have, in fact, been engaged in a fateful antagonism. While it has not yet taken the form of any shooting vis-à-vis the two principals, it has been well described as a cold war. *So far as national policies are concerned,* I think we have to conclude that we live in a time of war, not of peace. It follows that the current utilization of human resources must yield to the principle of national compulsion in place of that of voluntary participation.

If it is agreed that we are essentially in a time of war, the inescapable next question is: What measures of national compulsion in the utilization of human resources should we adopt? At the moment we are getting along with Selective Service, a system about which we learned a lot in World War II. In principle this system can be made to pick up all the able-bodied manpower there is if the national authorities so direct. However, Selective Service has become associated in the public mind with deferments and exemptions (as it properly may be so long as it is truly *selective*). Hence, certain authorities would have us believe that a more inclusive and drastic draft of manpower has become essential for our national protection and survival.

This view has been cogently presented by President Conant of Harvard. His concrete plan rests upon three stated assumptions, as follows: (1) only our Air Force and atom-bomb stockpile have kept Russia from attacking before now; (2) in the coming years, Russia's ability to attack with atom bombs and to defend her cities against our planes will increase rapidly; and (3) by 1952–54, Russia may consider that she has won the technological arms race and, if sure she can get to the Channel, will start a global war. Clearly enough it is the last of these assumptions which is most compelling.

President Conant admits that his assumptions may be challenged, but it is his contention that "as a guide to policy it would seem highly dangerous to proceed on any other basis than to assume that if there were no hazards from bombing and no hostility, the Russian expansion in the mid-1950's would involve Western Europe." It is apparently his conviction, as it is mine, that the survival of Western civilization will be determined in Europe rather than in Asia. He believes that it then follows: (1) "We in this country must assist in the rearmament of Western Europe." (2) "We must contribute a large force of American combat troops to be held in readiness in Europe." (3) "We must keep under arms three to three and one-half million men for years to come." Neither the present Selective Service system nor Universal Military Training seems to him to give promise of "accomplishing this immediate military objective." He concludes, therefore, that what we must have is a system of Universal Military Service under which "every young man on reaching the age of eighteen or on graduating from high school will be enrolled in the service of Uncle Sam for two years—the able-bodied to serve in the armed forces, those physically unfit to serve in other capacities at the same pay. There will be no deferments or exemptions for college students or anyone else."

The plan is as simple as that. Perhaps not quite so, for President Conant is familiar with the statistics and realizes that Universal Military Service for the eighteen- and nineteen-year-old boys alone will not create a fighting force of from three to three and one-half million men. He observes, therefore, that "recruiting will have to continue at a vigorous pace" and Selective Service will "have to be kept in reserve for use in event of a global war and possibly to supplement the universal service of the eighteen and nineteen-year age group." But upon the whole, the Conant plan is simplicity itself. That accounts in no small measure for its appeal. But the question remains: Are we dealing with a problem for which there is a simple and immediate solution; or, on the contrary, are we facing a situation which calls for measures of a complex and long-range character?

The answer to this question, I admit, depends upon what we believe the Russians are going to do. Are they planning for World War III by the mid-1950's? I have great difficulty myself in believing that they are. Of course, I realize that President Conant and others in high position may have information not available to the rest of us, but, taking such information as is generally available, there is a line of reasoning which I believe cannot safely be ignored.

There is little evidence that the Russians have been lacking in shrewdness or cunning since the conclusion of World War II. There is ample evidence, on the contrary, that they have been actually winning the cold war. Just why should they, now or in the early future, abandon the strategy they have been following so successfully? Why should they not, instead, keep the forces seeking world peace "off balance" and in a constant state of fear or even of panic? Why should they not create one crisis after another by exploiting the activities and ambitions of their satellites? Why should they not provoke a world-wide diversion of national resources to military preparedness, with the confident expectation that

153

this of itself will create the lower living standards on which Communism thrives? Why should they not keep on cultivating dissension and divisive forces wherever they appear? Why should they not do everything they can, short of outright war, to stimulate the development of authoritarianism throughout the world, with the idea that then the ultimate struggle will be between Fascism and Communism, and that the people, faced with only this choice, will take Communism? I can think of a score of reasons, only a few of which I have mentioned, which may lead the Russians to continue the cold war but to make sure that so far as they are concerned the cold war does not become World War III.

Of course, the Kremlin may lose its head, just as the war lords of Japan did in 1941. But thus far there are no signs of any creeping stupidity in the Kremlin maneuvers. Perhaps the Russians will pull a Pearl Harbor, but I credit them with more intelligence than that. Of course, too, the Russians may at some point miscalculate and start a shooting global war when they do not intend to do so. What I expect, however, is that they will keep right on doing what they have been doing so astutely since 1945. This may go on for decades. On the other hand, I realize, they *may* deliberately take steps which will precipitate World War III. We have to be prepared for either eventuality.

Under these conditions, what concretely shall *we* do? Shall we initiate a preventive war? In sheer logic it can be forcefully argued that if we are going to fight Russia inside of five years, we had better do it now. Doubtless, situations will arise in which we could find an excuse for starting hostilities—an excuse at least as good as that which put us into the Spanish-American War! As a matter of fact, it can reasonably be contended that we have such a situation in Korea right now. But the prevailing opinion of mankind, and certainly the overwhelming opinion of the American people, is dead set against the idea of a preventive war. There is no present indication that we and the other free nations of the world are disposed to initiate a global war now for a set of principles, however high and important the principles may be. When World War III comes, if it does, it will in all probability come because the *Russians,* overtly or otherwise, will start it. But will they go that far? On the assumption that we do not weaken, my own opinion is that the chances are that we are really in for a long protraction of the current so-called cold war.

If that is probably the kind of war we have to wage, how shall we fight it? Well, in general, we will fight it so far as we can with an eye on the basic values which have long characterized life in the United States. We will continue to build our phenomenal technological and industrial strength. We will do everything we possibly can to accelerate still further the extraordinary advances we have been making in science. We will strengthen our efforts to eradicate prejudice; to deal fairly with all groups of whatever color, creed, or national origin; to equalize opportunity; to establish justice and respect for law and order; to improve human relations, so as to create pervasive good will among men. We will seek in every way to realize more fully the ideals of freedom and democracy. We will develop and maintain a large and efficient military force. We will help other nations, not yet come under the Russian yoke, especially those in Western Europe, to gain strength and, as may be necessary, to re-arm. We will clarify and fortify the real voice of America. We will back the United Nations organization through thick and thin and with all the resources at our command. We

155

will gird our loins with a view to whatever emergency may arise, and commit ourselves to the idea that, world conditions being what they are, each one of us must render to the nation that service which will best serve the nation's interest.

For young men this total policy would appear to entail a period of compulsory Universal *National* Service. The period of service may well be two years, pending the appearance of proof that more than that is absolutely needed. Young women, where circumstances permit, should be encouraged to volunteer for a like period of service. Well, you may say, if this is the nature of the necessary commitment, why not the Conant plan?

My answer in general terms is that the Conant plan is *too* simple, and in consequence too rigid. I go along with the idea that we need a system of required National Service for all our young men between the ages of eighteen to twenty-six—two years of service, let us say. But let us make it a system of service which provides for enough flexibility of timing, assignment, and utilization, to make sure that: (1) a continued and actually increased flow of highly trained, scientific, scholarly, and professional personnel is maintained; (2) no substantial weakening of the necessary training institutions occurs; (3) the largest possible use of existing training facilities is made; (4) no avoidable disruption of our economy is precipitated—for example, in agriculture, through a loss of essential labor supply; (5) total costs are kept at a minimum; (6) military requirements are wisely co-ordinated with other paramount national needs (this may call for the creation of a supreme National Manpower Authority); (7) the advantages we have in our unparalleled industrial strength are further accentuated; (8) militarizing influences in our national civilian life are kept at a minimum; and (9) fundamental values in American life are not needlessly sacrificed.

It is my opinion that if we are in for a long struggle with the Russians and not for an early shooting war, adoption of the Conant plan will actually weaken our defenses. If I were in the Kremlin and were plotting a cold war lasting for decades, I would be pleased to have the American people adopt the Conant plan just as it stands. I would expect it, over the years, to keep the United States from developing to the full its possible powers. The Conant plan is sound only as it is short-range and provides for a quick and simple development of military forces. But in the long run, let us remember, we shall not defeat the Communists with sheer manpower. They are certain to outnumber us. If it is a long conflict that we face, surely the Conant plan in its present form is not the right answer. Wisely amended it might be something quite different.

President Conant has himself said of the plan he is proposing: "A great sacrifice in both general and liberal education and in professional training would be the consequence." He justifies this great sacrifice in terms of the "extreme peril" which he believes the free world now faces. However, the question remains: How is this extreme peril to be most effectively met? He remarks that "what we fail to do in 1950 may come home to roost in 1953." But it is equally true that what we do in 1950 may come home to roost in 1975. If we are on the brink of a shooting global war, of course "all bets are off"; then complete mobilization is in order. But if we are not to move into such an early,

157

shooting, global war, and may, instead, have to conduct a prolonged cold war, *long-range* planning is still of the essence of sound national policy.

President Conant has referred to his plan as involving "grim measures." The article presenting his plan is entitled, "A Stern Proposal for National Survival." Stern it surely is. But let us not forget that it is easier to be stern than it is to be wise. What we should be in our present dealings with Russia is tough *and* wise, not just tough. If the Russians can trick us into being unwisely tough, they will ultimately have their own way. Fortunately, this is not a probable outcome if we in the United States can keep our heads; for we have powers the Russians cannot match, powers derived from the freedoms the Communists seem unable to understand. Let them regiment as they will, time is on our side. Let us be of good courage. For the human spirit has an unalterable resistance to enslavement. At long last, sooner or later, freedom will achieve its final victory.

RESPONSIBILITY FOR
ENDURING VALUES

Facets of Freedom

I. Primary Elements of the American Tradition of Freedom

THE first element in the American tradition of freedom is: mankind craves freedom, and, given freedom, will use it responsibly. I suppose most Americans take this as a self-evident truth. Of course mankind craves freedom! As a matter of fact, in much of human experience, and certainly in our own individual lives, freedom is at times a rather terrifying thing. Surely it is often a most uncomfortable thing with which to live if we think of it as more than license to do what we choose. Clearly freedom is something very much more than that. Freedom implies responsibility. If you think of the two—freedom and responsibility—as always associated, you will see some of the questions that are raised when you say mankind craves freedom. In the American tradition, we have gone along with this proposition despite occasional misgivings. We believe men should be free. We believe that only through freedom can human hope and aspiration be realized.

Another element in the American tradition is equally fundamental: the judgment and conscience of the people can be trusted. This is occasionally questioned—sometimes

161

in high places. Obviously at times the people do go wrong; but if we are to fight for freedom, we must hold fast to this basic element of faith. We must believe that with knowledge the people will show vision; that, given power, they will assure justice. We Americans must stand for government of the people, for the people, and by the people.

The third proposition is historic: the rights of the state derive from the interests of the people. In other words, the state is an instrument with which the common good is promoted. It remains merely a means; back of it lies the end, the well-being of the people. This conception of the relationship between the people and the state dates from the very beginnings of orderly government on this continent. It is, in a sense, the very cornerstone of our political structure. The state is never supreme in American thought. The interest and the well-being of the people are what give the state its ultimate reason for existence.

The fourth proposition is closely related: the individual has rights which all government must respect. This is one of the elements of American political theory which people in other countries have most difficulty in understanding or accepting. It is an exceedingly important doctrine. There are certain rights of the individual which cannot be denied. These rights are inalienable; they belong to the very nature of man; they must be protected in whatever political system is operative.

The fifth proposition is this: popular education at public expense is indispensable in a democratic society. That, too, roots back to early times. One of the great early exponents was Jefferson. He has had many followers since, and the ideal has been greatly amplified. Now no longer challenged in principle, the question is how far the principle shall be extended. The common elementary school is in these days fully established. The common secondary school is increasingly accepted. It is quite likely that common public education will be extended even beyond this. Already, the American people have done more in the direction of free, popular education than any other people in the history of mankind. It is part of the American tradition that, with universal suffrage, universal education of the electorate is a necessary safeguard of a truly democratic system.

The sixth proposition is of wide relevance: the pursuit of truth, beauty, and goodness must not be subjected to political control. These are streams in the life of the people which must be kept completely uncontaminated by partisan interests. The pursuit of truth must be wholly untrammeled; it must be free to go where it will. We will undertake no ordering of beauty. There is no way of legislating goodness. All three are forces in human progress which must be left essentially free. These views have been basic in the American faith.

The seventh proposition is of increasing significance: science and technology hold the key to human progress. I put this into the list with certain reservations. It will be argued in some quarters that this is not of the same order as the others I have given, and that a great many people will not accept this as a valid American tradition. However, if one will examine the spirit of America over the last century and a half, one will see that science and technology have acquired tremendous prestige. We have come to have immeasurable confidence in what pure and applied science can do for us. We expect it to perform miracles of every description; we are constantly under its domination. What power the men of science wield! What influence they exert! In a sense, science has come to have possession of us; it is the one thing in which we have developed unquestioning faith. Increaseingly, I think, we have come to entertain the idea that, somehow or other, science and technology will in time give us what we would really like to have; it will actually implement the kind of human progress for which we are all so eager.

The eighth element of tradition has figured enormously in our American life: the common weal will be served through the competition of self-seeking private enterprises. We may have our doubts about certain individual undertakings, but we have retained an abiding faith in the effect of the whole constellation of competing enterprises. Working together, offsetting one another, compensating for one another, restraining one another, they result in a total system which we believe to be in the public interest. Over the years we have moderated the competitive system; we have imposed increasing regulations upon it; the fact remains that we have clung to the idea that the system remains essentially sound and may be expected to serve well the general welfare of all the people.

The ninth and last of the propositions is highly characteristic of the American tradition: the destiny of the American people lies in the hands of the American people. In other words, the future of the United States can be regarded as essentially self-determined, and not subject to serious interference from without. This idea we have had for long generations. The doctrine has been laid down in a series of official documents, some of them notable pronouncements of American policy. As a people we have clung to the doctrine right up to date. At the moment, we are beginning to have certain questions in our mind as to whether the proposition is one that can possibly be defended in the light of current events. But we have certainly believed in it in the past. To a consider-

164

able extent, I think, it is retained still by large sections of the American people. It certainly has to be mentioned in any attempt to explain the nature of the American tradition.

I would not for a moment claim that in these nine propositions I have stated all the principal elements in this American faith of ours. Doubtless I have omitted elements, and I am sure I have not given adequate explanation of some of those I have mentioned. Perhaps, however, the listing I have given will serve to focus attention on some of the issues which are most definitely involved in the present world conflict.

II. Wiser Tolerance

In the age-old quest for a better life, mankind has evolved certain ideas which are recognized as good by those who live in a democracy such as ours. Some of these ideas come immediately to mind: the idea of God, the idea of peace, the idea of justice, the idea of brotherhood, the idea of freedom, and the idea of tolerance. These ideas represent the better side of our nature as a people. While they are abstractions and are difficult to translate into terms of concrete social action, they stand as beacon lights along the way which our civilization must follow. They represent, in a sense, our hope of heaven in a world that is torn with discord after great and devastating wars.

To a considerable extent, these great guiding ideas are interdependent. Take, for example, the ideas of freedom and of tolerance. Surely one of the greatest of all blessings is freedom. We believe in all that freedom has to offer. Nevertheless, it is only a minority who think through all that freedom entails. The other face of the coin of freedom is responsibility,

165

individual and collective. The firm substance which joins freedom and responsibility is tolerance. Without tolerance, we evade a primary phase of the responsibility which freedom imposes. Without tolerance, there can, in fact, be no real freedom.

It is important when we speak of tolerance that we have a clear understanding of just what we are talking about. Tolerance is a frequently used word. It has a number of authentic meanings. These we need to distinguish. Tolerance may mean, for example, the ability to endure hardship and suffering. In this sense, Bacon says in one of his essays that "Diogenes, one terrible frosty morning, came to the market place and stood naked, quaking, to show his tolerance." Obviously this is not the sort of tolerance that we usually hold in high regard, and for all of his other admirable qualities, it is not likely that Diogenes would be accorded many laurels by a present-day audience for this kind of display of tolerance. He would be much more likely to wind up in the city jail or in the hands of a psychiatrist.

In medicine, tolerance is the inborn or acquired ability to handle a drug or a poison or some other substance taken into the human system. And so we speak of a man's tolerance of alcohol, thinking of the amount that he can imbibe without becoming either a medical problem or a public disgrace. Still a different sort of tolerance is involved when we come to consider the tolerance that society should, or should not, accord to alcoholics.

Again, tolerance may be used in a technical sense, connoting a permissible deviation from a specified standard. Thus, an engineer may speak of a mechanical part which has a diameter of one inch (the standard), with a tolerance of $\frac{1}{100}$ of an inch (the permissible deviation). Not all machine parts can be perfect in measure. Tolerance is the margin of error within which they may pass inspection.

This brings us to a consideration of tolerance in the sense that we most frequently have in mind when we use the word. When we say that someone is tolerant, we are usually referring to a very admirable charactertistic or habit of mind: making allowance for the existence of beliefs or practices that are different, displaying freedom from bigotry, understanding the beliefs of others without necessarily sharing them. Obviously there is some relationship between this particular kind of tolerance and the other kinds that I mentioned. Tolerance is an attribute of the open, understanding mind, which may, under certain circumstances, involve one in the suffering of Diogenes, although suffering that may not be so unabashed in its setting. Tolerance in men, as in machines, involves recognition of certain differences, or deviations from standard, that is essential for making democracy work.

These differences lead naturally to one of the most perplexing questions that we have to face in the field of human relationships: can we have too much tolerance? All of us would agree that there are areas in which an excess of tolerance will never be a danger. We cannot have too much appetite for new learning or too much zest in honest inquiry. At the very heart of a great university lies the untrammeled pursuit of truth. We cannot here wisely impose restrictions upon the acquiring of knowledge and its dissemination. In short, we must stand in a university for great tolerance of new ideas and of previously untraveled lines of thought.

In times of uncertainty and confusion, when anxieties of all sorts are abroad, this practice of open-minded thinking is not easily maintained. All sorts of prejudices threaten it. All sorts of pressure groups undertake to throttle it. But if history tells us anything at all about the progress of civilization, it tells us that attempts to check the search for truth have never benefited mankind, and in the long run have never succeeded. No educational institution in a free society can call its soul its own if it fails to tolerate differences of opinion honestly and intelligently held. Nothing short of this is consistent with a genuine love of truth.

Similarly, we cannot have too much tolerance of those differences of human form and origin which have no relevance to personal character and capacity. In this area we stand face to face with some of the most persistent of human prejudices. All through the ages there have been deep-seated reactions in human society to variations of sex, race, creed, and color. These reactions have stood in the way of human relations based solidly on considerations of individual worth. We say all men are created free and equal. As matters stand, they certainly are not. With respect to many qualities men never will be equal in promise or in status. But surely we should strive to establish conditions under which all have equal chances of realizing fully the potentialities they individually possess. This we can accomplish only as we eradicate some of the prejudices which now play so large a part in human affairs. Here is an area in which we desperately need more tolerance than we yet exhibit. Educational institutions should take the lead in breaking down the instinctive prejudices which result in "man's inhumanity to man."

I have just given two simple examples of areas in which the need for greater tolerance is unchallenged by any who understand the essentials of our democracy. There are other areas in which lines are not so clearly drawn, where it appears that we are disposed already to exhibit too much tolerance. The public attitude toward safety on the highways is a case in point. Most of us know the difference between proper and improper handling of an automobile. A conspicuous few either don't know or don't care. As a result, thousands of lives are needlessly lost each year. A very few states, notably Pennsylvania, have adopted, as an expression of public will, legislation designed to curb reckless driving. Throughout most of the country, however, the people of the several states have declined to adopt what might seem to be repressive measures, and the toll continues to be frightful. I suppose that in some quarters this attitude on the part of the public might be described as a manifestation of tolerance, a desire not to restrict the rights of our fellow citizens to take chances even at the risk of killing others.

Another example of what might appear on the surface to be tolerance is our attitude toward the family and the accessory institution of divorce. I suppose that none of us would presume to sit in judgment on the moral issues involved in every case of a broken home with which we are acquainted. The simple fact is that we are all acquainted with too many of them. We know that the divorce rate is climbing rapidly, leaving tens of thousands of children without the decent start toward citizenship that a home affords. What are we doing about it? Obviously we are not doing much; and what we are doing, we are not doing with any marked degree of success. Does this mean that we are being tolerant of those who lack the moral stamina to accept the responsibility which they incurred in marriage? If this is tolerance, it would certainly appear to be excessive.

We can think of parallel examples in the student life of a university, where questions of manners, habits, and general conduct on the part of a minority are occasionally an issue. Andrew Dickson White tells a story of the early years of

Cornell University which involved a plea for a rather special sort of tolerance. In the words of President White:

> Several of the young women who first applied for admission held high ideas as to their rights. To them Sage College was an offense. Its beautiful parlors, conservatories, library, lecture-rooms, and lawns, with its lady warden who served as guide, philosopher, and friend, were all the result of a deep conspiracy against the rights of women. Again and again a committee of them came to me, insisting that young women should be treated exactly like young men; that there should be no lady warden; that every one of them should be free to go and come from Sage College at every hour in the twenty-four, as young men were free to go and come from their dormitories. My answer was that the cases were not the same; that when young women insisted on their right to come and go at all times of the day and night, as they saw fit, without permission, it was like their right to walk from the campus to the beautiful point opposite us on the lake: the right they undoubtedly had, but insurmountable obstacles were in the way; and I showed them that a firm public opinion was an invincible barrier to the liberties they claimed.

The difference between the sort of tolerance which the young ladies requested, and which was obviously not in their interests or in the interests of the University, and the sort of tolerance which we extend, for example, to people of other religious faiths becomes clearer. In asking to be allowed to go against the accepted social and educational principles of their day, the young ladies at Sage were asking not for tolerance, as they imagined, but for indulgence. Our attitude toward reckless driving becomes, in this light, not one of tolerance, but of indulgence, and so do our attitudes toward certain broad social problems, and some of our attitudes toward morals and manners.

170

In still another area, the question of tolerance is profoundly important for all of us. I refer to the area in which we are faced with the *methods* of effecting social and political change. Here issues of tolerance challenge all of the intelligence we can muster. Speaking broadly, social progress is accomplished in two ways, peacefully or through resort to war, by evolution or through revolution. In America we are irrevocably committed to one of these ways, and just as completely opposed to the other. We have established constitutional procedures under which the will of the people can express itself without resort to violence. Those who assert that social change can be brought about in America only through resort to revolutionary practices are challenging not only our form of government but our very way of life.

Communism, as opposed to democracy in America, is not only a type of economic organization, but a way of seeking change. It is a way that frankly avows relentless warfare and asserts that in war "all is fair." Deceit, chicanery, treachery are employed by Communism as appropriate means of confusing the opposition and dividing its "enemy." Communism considers honesty, integrity, and conscience to be evidences of "bourgeois" weakness and decadence. It looks upon honor as an effete possession of those who still think that freedom, good will, and peace are among life's greatest blessings.

To what degree should we tolerate Communism in this country? The answer is plain: toward practices of the sort Communism inculcates we should display no tolerance whatsoever. They poison the very springs of the human relationships we must retain and cultivate. If we would keep our democracy, we have no option but to insist upon certain ways of effecting social change: ways established in our governmental system, embedded in our national tradition,

171

and fought and bled for by countless Americans living and dead. Every one of us must recognize that there are honest and dishonest ways of doing business together. Only as we come to deal honestly with one another are we likely to survive as a free people.

Now someone may ask how we are to reconcile intolerance of Communism with civil liberties. My answer here is that no question of civil liberties is involved, since we are not proposing to deprive anyone of liberties under the Bill of Rights. We are dealing with an ideology. This ideology, if given the concrete form of government, would deprive us of the liberties which we hold most dear. We should fight it with every means at our disposal under the Constitution which it seeks to destroy.

From all this it appears that the cultivation of tolerance is not a simple undertaking. Some things we should tolerate more, much more than we do; other things we should tolerate less; some not at all. In short, the wise cultivation of tolerance is a difficult business, for it involves an exacting balance between too little and too much. Most people tend to become habitually tolerant or intolerant; few are intelligently now one, now the other. Not that vacillation between tolerance and intolerance is a virtue, but wise discrimination in demonstrating one or the other certainly is. In other words, tolerance should be a reflection of something deeper. It should reflect the requirements of freedom, and freedom itself lacks point and direction except as guiding moral and spiritual principles come into play.

III. *The Defense of Freedom*

The cold war in which we are now engaged with Russia is but the sharp focus of a wider image—the image of conflicting ideologies with which human affairs are currently beset.

The cold war we can see clearly enough. It spells itself out in a multi-billion-dollar-a-year military defense program, in a multi-billion-dollar-a-year European economic recovery program, in the dramatic showing of our forces in the Berlin Airlift, in endless, frustrating debates in the meetings of the United Nations, in an accumulation of atomic bombs.

But behind all this is a war of ideas and ideals.

It is oversimplification to say that this ideological war relates wholly to the struggle between Communism and democracy. It cuts more deeply than this. It has to do with basic conceptions of social progress, political organization, and human relationships. It poses such fundamental questions as these:

How much can the material lot of mankind be improved while freedom is retained? What are the social requisites of freedom? What, after all, is freedom worth?

These are questions which no immediate improvement of our relationships with the present Soviet regime will dismiss. The rise and continuation of dictatorships all over the world give some of the answers. These dictatorships constitute part of the fighting front opposing us. They serve to identify the immense responsibility of free America in shaping the destiny of mankind for generations to come. They serve to accentuate the stresses and strains with which we are internally afflicted.

173

We are in a war, true enough, but it is a war more significantly related to our way of life than to our military and economic might. *It is, in essence, a life and death struggle of ideas and ideals.*

This conflict of ideologies will not be resolved by the intellectual, but by the common man, asserting his newly acquired powers.

A profound change has come over human affairs since the turn of the century. We are now witnessing the effects in combination of three great social developments: widening suffrage, popular education, and perfection of the techniques of modern mass communication. The net result of these developments has been a transfer of unprecedented power to the masses. Great groups of men and women, acting in concert, have acquired command of practices with which to make their potential powers effective. As is almost invariably true, these unaccustomed powers are in some quarters being abused. There is much about the current situation which seems ominous.

The fact remains that the transformation we have seen the world over in the position and play of the common people is not likely to be displaced, short of dictatorship. *The future of freedom is really now in the custody of the common man.*

If the preservation of freedom has become a charge of the common man, it follows that the common man must acquire knowledge commensurate with his present responsibilities.

We pride ourselves on the literacy of the American people, and well we may. But it is still a literacy primarily related to the three R's. With respect to such subjects as history, government, economics, psychology, health, and ethics, the lack

174

of knowledge and understanding among the people is abysmal and threatening.

To what extent does the man on the street have any real awareness of the requisites of popular rule and stable self-government, of the administration of justice, and the importance of the maintenance of law and order? To what extent does he realize the significance in our economy of private initiative, of the sustained flow of venture capital, of good workmanship and high productivity on the part of labor, of the profit motive as a prime mover in any free competitive system? To what extent does he see the inescapable connections between, on the one hand, collective freedom and, on the other hand, individual honesty, tolerance, charity, courage, and honor? These are matters of understanding without which the people may lose their freedom out of sheer ignorance.

Herein lie tremendous responsibilities for education.

As a people, we have been taking democracy almost entirely for granted. We have been blithely assuming that human progress by its very nature leads in the direction of freedom and democracy. That whole idea is now under sharp attack. *As never before, we need to think more earnestly about the real meaning of democracy in America.*

Let us not forget that the basic documentation of our American way of life was shaped in a radically different kind of society. The United States in the late eighteenth century was a rural, agricultural, sparsely populated nation, scattered in large part along the Atlantic seaboard. Look at it today—dominantly urban, tremendously industrialized, populated beyond the wildest dreams of the Founding Fathers, taking in the better part of the whole North American continent.

The drafters of the Declaration of Independence, the Federal Constitution, and the first great amendments to that amazing document could quite properly direct their attention to the *rights* of free men in the great self-governing republic. They had just won their freedom. They would write it into enduring law. They did so with marvelous wisdom, and we; their successors, are everlastingly indebted to them.

What the Founding Fathers did not do, however, was to identify the *responsibilities,* individual and collective, which go along with the rights they established. *Freedom, though priceless, is not to be had for nothing.*

For example, it is one thing to enjoy freedom of speech; it is something else to respect its obligations. We can all see that no one has the right to cry "fire!" in a crowded theater when there is no fire. But what about appeals to passion and prejudice, when reason and fair-mindedness are what the common weal requires? And what about the right of assembly, if it is used indirectly to plot the overthrow through violence of constituted and fairly elected authorities?

These are simply examples of what I have in mind when I assert that we greatly need in the United States a more extended and explicit definition of the essential ingredients of the American way of life. We need this in answer to the attack to which our great tradition is being subjected. We need it in terms of the complicated workaday world in which Americans carry on. *We need it in terms of the responsibilities without which our rights cannot be permanently retained.*

To give the American people the knowledge essential to the preservation of their freedom, education in all its branches, formal and informal, must bring to bear every resource at its command. All the various instruments must be employed. All the diverse agencies must participate. New teaching devices, such as the films, radio, and television, must certainly be applied. The co-operation of the great mass media is needed. *Only if the people, by every available means, are given new knowledge, can they come to see clearly how their liberties are to be securely defended.*

Knowledge alone will not suffice: there is a self-discipline of free men without which freedom cannot possibly be sustained.

It is at this point that we touch the greatest issue of all. Can men and women who are essentially free sufficiently subordinate their individual interests to the well-being of all? If in possession of power, can they see the necessity of exercising it for the common good? Can they be led to show generosity toward the less privileged, and compassion toward the victims of destructive circumstances? Can they be persuaded to resist all influences which appeal to avarice, envy, and covetousness? Can they be made to display courage in the face of frustration and failure? Can they successfully establish in their inner drives the practice of unflagging personal integrity? Can they, short of war, come to have an adequate sense of common purpose?

These are not just rhetorical questions. They are fundamental issues in human destiny. The answer given by the dictators is an absolute "No"; there follows the resort to authoritarian forms of rule. The equally positive answer of the true democrats is "Yes." Only time can say whether our faith is justified.

What we do know already is that the present world conflict is essentially a struggle of fundamentally opposed social disciplines.

177

On the one hand is the discipline of the dictatorship. It is a forced, regimented, authoritarian discipline. It is harsh, callous, ruthless, utterly demanding.

In striking contrast, the foundations of the discipline of the free or democratic society lie deep in human hope and aspiration. This is the discipline which builds, not in fear of suffering and misfortune, but in the promise of greater happiness and well-being. The values toward which it endeavors to direct the larger powers which flow from social discipline are those which reside in a broad and expanding humanitarianism. It finds no place for treachery and cynicism. It believes in peace. It has a great and enduring faith in mankind. It is a discipline that is responsible and self-imposed. *Without this sort of discipline, freedom is doomed to self-destruction.*

In the final defense of freedom, there is no substitute for the love of truth.

If history tells us anything, it is that knowledge is power, and that mankind has never been betrayed by fresh accessions of truth.

We live in a period of appalling confusion. We are harried by all sorts of doubts and fears. Our emotions having been deeply disturbed, our capacity for clear reasoning is, for the time being, impaired. In consequence, we are striking out rather blindly against certain of the forces we resist.

The actions we are taking in the field of higher education are a case in point. The elimination of avowed members of the Communist Party from our educational institutions would seem to be fully warranted. The faculty of any college or university should be made up of free, honest, competent, inquiring minds which seek to find and disseminate the truth. The mind of a member of the Communist Party is a fettered mind, enslaved to the party line. It cannot possibly claim to be free and honest. It is manifestly disqualified for membership in a faculty of higher learning in a free and freedom-loving society such as ours.

But in undertaking to eliminate these traitors to the American academic tradition, we must be careful not to sacrifice free and inquiring minds that are honestly engaged in the pursuit of truth, however disturbing this truth may appear to be. Professors are by nature, it has been said, individuals who think otherwise. Some of them are a bit queer. All I have known are extraordinarily honest. All of them are exceedingly individualistic. The last thing in the world they would do is to sacrifice freedom. They play an invaluable role in a society such as ours. We must make sure that we do not hamstring their invaluable activities. *The untrammeled pursuit of truth, wherever it may take us, is an indispensable part of any long-range defense of freedom.*

The most serious threats to freedom in America are not overt, but insidious, and must be dealt with as such.

The fundamental threats to freedom are not likely to appear in sudden crises, posing issues clearly and unmistakably. No free people ever gave up its freedom wittingly or willingly. Certainly the American people never will. The real threats may, though this is not likely, come to us in the setting of war. We have demonstrated that we know how to deal with external aggression. Our tremendous military and economic power remains unchallenged. Should we find ourselves once more driven into armed conflict, the next war will not find us unprepared or unable to defend ourselves.

But processes of insidious corrosion may, in time, undermine our strength. We may lose our customary spirit of adventure. We may come to place undue emphasis on in-

179

dividual security and purely material prosperity. It is against dangers of this sort that we must guard. It is no secret that there is a natural aging in civilizations. Every successful civilization hitherto known has in time developed its own degenerative diseases. We know that these can take the form of complacency, apathy, ease, and excessive self-interest. Can we avoid these in our own America? We can if, *as a people,* we have the vision and the will. To the forces which shape our ideas and ideals, this is the supreme challenge.

If all this reads like a sermon, the reader must charge that in part to me, and in part to the nature of education. For education is like religion. It is a light by which the path of human progress is illumined. When darkness descends and there is no vision, the people perish. When the lights are dimmed and vision is obscured, the people lose their freedom. Let us, one and all, do all within our power, individually and collectively, to make sure that the lights do not burn low, and that the vision we must have is never lost.

Qualities of Democratic

Leadership

As we view the world in which we live, it is all too apparent that it is a divided world. In fact, this is currently its most conspicuous feature. We may have moved into *one* world, but it is obviously one world in *two* parts. On the one side, there is the USSR; on the other, the USA. On the one side, there is an aggressive Communism; on the other, a vigorous capitalism. On the one side, there is government by dictatorship; on the other, government by free election. For the time being these two parts of the world are so profoundly in opposition in both theory and practice that there seems to be no way in which to effect any reconciliation of their conflict. Hence we are in what has come to be known as a cold war. This we may think of as the most striking feature of the present world outlook.

But a more significant description of the world we now have is that it is a world in transition. Profound changes in the organization of human affairs have been under way for at least half a century. As a matter of fact, these changes can be identified over a much longer period. They are the changes which stem from the wide extension of popular education and the suffrage. We are at last witnessing the

181

effects of the expanding forces and advancing techniques of mass communication as represented in public education, the news service and periodicals, the motion picture, radio, and television. Common people the world over are becoming informed and articulate, and are taking hold.

To a considerable extent the nature and scope of this profoundly important movement have been obscured by the two world wars which have been fought within the past thirty-five years. Attention has naturally been focused on the devastating effects of these stupendous conflicts. Inevitably such periods of organized destruction turn the spotlight on certain economic disturbances, such as the radical dislocation of world trade, the phenomenal increase of governmental indebtedness, the collapse of monetary systems, the disruptive inflationary movements which inevitably accompany any life-and-death struggle of the nations. We tend to think of rising costs, in particular of the high cost of living, and of increasing taxes. Inflation can play havoc with customary economic relationships, as well as with established social institutions. The private institutions of this country —the hospitals, social agencies, churches, colleges, and universities—are in serious distress as a result of the complications which inflation has injected into their financial affairs. Thus, wars have a way of unsettling the social order as well as effecting great political realignments.

But underneath the social, economic, and political impact of these world wars is the broader and deeper social movement to which I have alluded. Massive activities now challenge the established social order. I repeat, the common people are coming into unprecedented power. They have been learning the lessons of effective organization. They are

182

making themselves heard; they are asserting their will as never before.

This we can observe all over the world. In some countries it is showing itself in the form of insistent demands for national independence. In other countries it is appearing in revolutionary movements designed to upset and displace the established governments. In countries like our own, which happily have long since made provision for peaceful change in response to the demands of the people, the same forces are expressing themselves in the widespread drive for the establishment of the so-called welfare state.

Every society and every movement has its leaders. There are those leaders—dictators—who have captured the techniques of modern propaganda, using them to suffocate the will of the majority, and impose instead the domination of a ruthless minority. These dictators follow the theory that the state is supreme. In these states the citizens are given an excited sense of mass dedication to political and social ends, which they themselves have not helped to define, and which they do not need to understand in order to accept.

Then there is a leadership which does not seek to dominate, but seeks instead, through the use of liberal institutions, to carry into effect the best aspirations of the entire body of active and free citizens. This we call democratic leadership.

In the difference between these forms of leadership we can discern the nature of the conflict with which all mankind is now confronted.

Never was there a time in which the qualities of truly democratic leadership were more critically important. Except as the common people are wisely led, the will of the

183

people may be worked in such a way as ultimately to wreck their own interests. We face, therefore, the necessity of getting, certainly in a country dedicated as ours is to the principles of democratic rule, a clear understanding of the contributions which leadership must make if America is to remain both prosperous and free.

Clearly enough, leadership must do something more than merely reflect prevailing popular thought and ambition. I say this because I am convinced that the mass of the people need guidance. Leadership must serve to raise the general level of understanding and intelligence. It must strive to make the thinking of the people sound and realistic. It must undertake to teach as it leads. For example, it must endeavor to give the people an understanding of the fundamental fact that what is not produced cannot be consumed; that to be strong and prosperous, a people must create and produce. Over the years there is no substitute for productive work—hard and sustained productive work—if the necessary economic base for political and social advances is to be established and maintained.

Of course, democratic leadership must be sensitive and sympathetic to the needs of the people. It cannot afford to be cynical about human hopes and ideals. It cannot gain or retain power if it is patently cold and calculating. But, while it is warm and responsive, it must stand firmly against those drives which ignore the common weal. More and more we witness today the activity of pressure groups which seek to promote their own interests. More and more the majority are being pushed about by militant minorities. It is obvious that the special interests of these pressure groups when added together do not assure the well-being of all. Furthermore, the inescapable consequence of the activity of these special-interest pressure groups is to induce chronic contention and increasing divisiveness in public affairs. Somewhere in the total situation there must be wise and courageous spokesmen for the common core of interests which determine the long-range prosperity and happiness of the people as a whole. Democratic leaders must defend at all costs the broader and more inclusive interests which will surely stand the test of time.

It is one of the great responsibilities of democratic leadership to resist the forces of passion, deception, and prejudice which afflict us all. It is only as democratic leadership raises the level of public thought and feeling above these weaknesses of our everyday life that we may expect in time truly to establish democracy. For democracy is not only a system of government; it is a moral order as well. There are certain enduring moral virtues without which freedom and culture cannot possibly be assured. There are no substitutes in a free society for common honesty, personal integrity, and an unswerving devotion to truth. Democratic leaders must be outstanding exemplars of the kind of individual discipline without which free men cannot expect to remain free.

In short, there are certain fundamental requisites for wise and resolute democratic leadership. It must build on hope, not on fear; on honesty, not on falsehood; on justice, not on injustice; on public tranquility, not on violence; on freedom, not on enslavement. It must weave a social fabric in which the most important strands are devotion to truth and commitment to righteousness. These are absolutely essential ingredients of the American way of life. They are the necessary conditions for the achievement of freedom and human progress the world over.

The democratic leader who exhibits these qualities will

185

have no lust for power. He will not rejoice in victory over his rivals, save as victory advances the humane cause he espouses. He will meet the requirements of his office in a humility born of an acute awareness of his great public responsibilities. With Abraham Lincoln, he will say, "As I would not be a slave, so I would not be a master." With the ancient Prophet, he will do justly, love mercy, and walk humbly with his God.

There is no short and easy road to the heights of human aspiration. This the people must come to realize. This their leaders must help them to see. Leaders and followers alike must know that only as there is a discipline of body, mind, and spirit will free men and women gain the rewards which life at its best has to offer.

In a democracy leadership comes from all parts of society. But our universities and colleges are an especially rich source of the leadership we need. Upon them rests, therefore, a solemn charge: the obligation to teach that true leadership in a democracy is always a moral office, and that it owes its fundamental allegiance to all humanity in the eternal search for greater liberty, greater happiness, and lasting peace.

Of Loyalties

EFFECTIVE loyalties may be thought of as in three categories: personal, institutional, and ideational. Personal loyalties are those we feel toward individuals we know, or think we know. Institutional loyalties are those we develop toward all the diverse organizations to which we belong: the club, the fraternity or sorority, the college or university, the state or nation. Ideational loyalties are those we come to acknowledge to certain ideas and ideals, such as justice or democracy.

How are these different types of loyalty interrelated? To what extent are they complementary, to what extent competing? Are there among them any definite priorities? On what basis do we determine which come first? Is there rationing to be done in terms of their relative claims? These are questions which a life-and-death struggle, such as that in which we are engaged, compels us to consider and, in so far as possible, to answer. With this in view, let us look more carefully into these groupings into which our loyalties so clearly fall.

Personal loyalties are basic in all human experience. Among such personal loyalties, the most basic of all is our loyalty to ourselves. We start developing that at a very early age. The small infant who bites his toe till it hurts and thereafter desists is learning loyalty to himself at a very rudi-

187

mentary level. Gradually the conception of self expands. It covers the whole complicated body mechanism that lies at our disposal. It comprehends our unfolding intellectual and spiritual life. It carries our hopes and fears, our wants and ambitions. It finally involves us in a paramount loyalty to our own best selves. There are no loyalties quite so important as those that lie in a fully developed sense of individual integrity.

The loyalties to ourselves which begin to form at a very early age are associated almost from the start with personal loyalties toward those upon whom we are dependent. The mother-child relationship is the largest single source of these initial, personal attachments; but the circle soon widens. Father, brothers and sisters, playmates, schoolmates get included. The radiation continues: college classmates, husbands and wives, neighbors, fellow club members, fellow citizens, fellow workers, heroes and heroines of all sorts, professional colleagues, political leaders. There is no end to the range which personal loyalties may take. They may even go so far as to involve the idolatrous worship of a *Fuehrer*.

Our most concrete and intimate loyalties are all personal loyalties. No other loyalties are so constantly with us; no others tend so persistently to dominate us. With some people, personal loyalties are the only ones that really count. With every one of us, they are profoundly important.

Under modern social conditions, institutional loyalties are just about as pervasive. We are all caught in a great mesh of organizations of every description. Some are formal; others, informal. Some are economic in purpose; others, religious or educational; still others, political; some, purely social. The strength of the ties they entail varies enormously. College loyalties, for example, are sometimes very strong; at other times, manifestly weak. Loyalty to the party in

188

American political life has had a tremendous influence. The most significant single example of institutional allegiance is loyalty to the nation. Patriotism for centuries has been, and doubtless for centuries to come will remain, one of the greatest of all social forces. In general, institutional loyalties permeate human affairs and have a vast deal to do with the course of human events.

Over the ages, however, the loyalties which transcend all others are those which relate to certain great ideas and ideals. Human progress without loyalties of this order would be impossible. They are what keep mankind at its never-ending quest for truth, beauty, justice, good will, brotherhood. At times these great ideals seem remote and unattainable. Certainly at times they seem to be defied, if not wholly defeated. The fact remains that they alone over countless generations have kept alive the aspiring spirit of man. It is in fidelity to these more enduring ideals of life that individual as well as social undertakings find their final satisfaction and meaning.

If we thus review our loyalties we are forced to certain conclusions. Personal loyalties are basic. They give color and content to our daily living. They are the molecules of which our larger relationships are composed. Life without them would be quite untenable. But the purpose and the pattern of life need to be set by larger considerations than can be encompassed by any individual, be he great or small. Personal loyalties, essential though they be, find their validation in loyalties of a more inclusive sort.

Institutional loyalties are clearly a social necessity. Anarchy and social chaos can be avoided only through social organization, and such organization could not function if it did not elicit loyalties. The purposes served by social organizations vary enormously, however, and so do the corresponding loyalties. Allegiance to an exclusive club may serve primarily to nourish personal pride and a sense of social status. The same may be true of school or college connections. The fact that an organization is reputable does not prove that its contributions are worth while. Institutional loyalties should be constantly reviewed and evaluated. They need to be checked against loyalties of a higher order.

These higher loyalties are to be found among the loyalties which relate to the great and enduring ideals which have guided mankind through the ages. These are the loyalties which should govern our personal and institutional attachments. Only when our personal and institutional loyalties complement and reinforce our ideational loyalties can we be sure that our system of individual allegiance is firmly based.

In some ways, our ideational loyalties may seem abstract, remote, and futile. It is our job to make them concrete, intimate, and effective. We can live truth if we set out to do so. We can strive to expel error and prejudice. We can resolve to spread no report the accuracy of which we have reason to question. We can seek the facts when they are available. Living truthfully will make a positive difference in our daily lives. Once we get really exercised in justice, we can do a lot about that, too, here and now. If we come *really* to believe in good will and brotherhood, in kindly, considerate, understanding human relationships, we can do a great deal more than we have done to put them into effect in home and school, in neighborhood and community, in shop and trade, in the nation and throughout the world.

190

A Word on Behalf

of American Youth

BOLD, indeed, would be the man who undertook to speak authoritatively for American youth; for a man to speak for American youth may appear to be plainly presumptuous. Nevertheless, that is what I propose to do. Adult life may have its disadvantages in this connection, but many years of association with school and college youth should have off-setting advantages. Fortified with such confidence as may be drawn from this long and wide acquaintance with young people, I am going to act as youth's spokesman, bringing to your attention certain views which, I have every reason to believe, are much on the minds of a host of young people in America today.

There are at least three good reasons for undertaking this rather difficult task. In the first place, youth is badly handicapped in getting its views effectively before the American public. Youth is relatively unorganized. Youth has not learned to operate through pressure groups. On many subjects it appears to be strangely inarticulate. Thus far it has not had effective access to the instruments of propaganda. Here and there the voice of youth is being heard; by and large, even when raised, it is drowned in the clamor of other parties. It is time to make an effort to give youth a chance to have its say.

In the second place, it is clear that a somewhat sharper competition of age groups looms in the immediate future of American life. Already in some states the question has arisen whether old-age pensions or public school costs are going to be covered by the diminishing public funds that are available. There is every reason to think that the aged and infirm will make increasing demands upon the national income. Evidence accumulates that the adult population will increasingly restrict the opportunities for youthful employment in industry. In still another quarter, a steadily rising burden of benefits for the veterans of the wars promises to draw divisive lines of interests between our age groups. More and more it becomes clear that among the stresses and strains of the present social order are those which stem not from the conflicts of classes but from the competing interests of the successive generations.

The changing age composition of the American population is almost certain to accentuate all this. As the fundamental shift in the age composition of our population takes place, the competing interests of the generations may be expected to become more and more sharply drawn. Under these circumstances it is important that measures be adopted to secure more effective presentation of the desires and interests of our young people.

In the third place, I venture to act as spokesman for American youth because I believe it to be one of the privileges of the teaching profession to serve as mediator between each oncoming generation and those that have gone before. In times of relative economic stability and little social change, the reconciliation of the differences between the generations is not likely to prove troublesome. But in times like our own, in which profoundly important changes are taking place with disconcerting speed, age groups separated by no more than fifteen or twenty years may live in totally unsympathetic worlds. The adult population has been too engrossed in its own troubles to give much heed to the correlative perplexities and difficulties of youth. Herein lies a part of the opportunity and the obligation of the great company of educators: to make more widely known the interests and aspirations of American youth in the troubled times through which we are passing.

It has to be admitted at the outset that, with reason, youth might have a sharply critical attitude toward the legacy of our times. From the perspective of today, here is a bitter, almost ridiculous irony about the idea that the wars were fought "to end all wars" or "to make the world safe for democracy." The current deterioration of international morality and the constant threat of further wars are both appallingly evident. Within our own country the national economy remains sadly confused. A mounting public debt poses to youth the problem of later repayment. The natural resources upon which the national economy is based are not what they used to be, with free land gone, forest land largely denuded, millions of tons of topsoil washed to the sea, and mineral deposits substantially reduced. No, youth would be within its rights if it commented rather caustically upon the job which has been done by its predecessors. Upon the whole, the attitude which youth has taken with regard to these matters is extraordinarily free of resentment. Happily, youth concentrates its attention on the future, not on the past.

The significant views of American youth as it looks at its future relate to a wide variety of subjects, many of which I cannot undertake to consider. I propose to confine my reporting to the views of American youth with regard to the schools, security, democracy, and world peace. These are all very large subjects, and all I can hope to do is to give in barest outline some of the views which I believe American youth to be entertaining.

1. The attitude of youth toward the schools has been profoundly affected by the fact that the secondary school, as well as the elementary, has become well-nigh inescapable. Time was—and not so very long ago—when those who did not like formal education could avoid it after a limited sentence in the elementary grades; there was always some kind of a job to which to escape. That time seems to have passed, with little if any prospect of its return. It now looks as if, up to age eighteen, or possibly nineteen or twenty, young people in America will be compelled to go to some kind of school. The high school can no longer be thought of as a school for the more academically disposed minority of young Americans; it has become a school for all young Americans of whatever disposition.

The attitude of youth toward the schools is widely variant, of course, and reflects a great diversity of youthful interests, attitudes, and aspirations. It is safe to say, however, that by the time they are well along in their teens, the great bulk of our young people wish to have school programs exhibit clear and fairly direct bearing upon the life interests of the learners. What are some of the primary roles these young people expect shortly to be playing? Obviously they wish to become workers or producers, in other words, job-holders; the great bulk of them wish to become home- and family-builders; less uniformly and less fervently, they wish to be effective citizens. Here are approaching responsibilities for

194

which they would like to prepare. They are not inclined to accept the doctrine that no specific preparation is in order; that the only suitable course of training is indirect and is solely concerned with the cultivation of intellectual and moral virtues.

No thoughtful person is going to question the importance of these intellectual and moral virtues. No one is suggesting that society try to dispense with these virtues. On the contrary, everyone wants a more ample supply of them, and the only serious question is how to get it. One answer is to return to the traditional academic disciplines; the other is to reorganize the curriculum with specific reference to the evolving life interests of the learners. It is reasonably clear that youth leans to the latter view of the matter. By some this is thought to be due to a softening of the intellectual and moral fiber of youth. Frankly, it does not seem to me that this is a fair interpretation. We must realize that the secondary school is dealing with a new kind of school population, and that young Americans of secondary-school age are facing a new kind of world. It would be surprising, indeed, if under these circumstances, no change of school program were in order.

Youth, then, is somewhat critical of the American school of today and is looking, rather confidently, I believe, for certain changes for the better. Without seeking any softening of the school program, youth expects the American school of the future to cope more successfully with vocational training and adjustment, with preparation for home and family life, with training for effective citizenship in a truly democratic America. Here is a challenge from youth to the schoolmen that cannot be brushed aside.

One further idea about education gains wider and wider circulation among our young people. Increasingly it is held

195

that individuals of promise should not be kept from realizing their promise through lack of financial means. It is argued, and soundly so, that there is inexcusable social as well as individual waste in our failure to provide means by which gifted young Americans can obtain full development. Some system of wise selection and subsequent financial aid should be devised and supported. Where are those who will seriously question the soundness of this proposal?

2. Given employment, what does American youth expect of its future? In the first place, it does not look for opportunities to accumulate large means; it recognizes that the day of the great American fortune has passed, probably never to return. But as an offset, a measurable increase in security is looked for; in fact, demanded. At times it would appear as if American youth had grown prematurely old in its insistence upon guaranties of security rather than upon chances for adventure. Presumably this attitude springs from fear that the chances of successful adventure have ceased to be reasonable. For the time being American youth is disillusioned. For it the glamor of life is in eclipse. But the spirit of adventure which always lies latent in youth will return to life. After all, the world remains an extraordinarily interesting place. Science and technology continue to perform their miracles, and thrilling careers of invention and discovery remain open. Service to one's times still carries its rich rewards. The opportunities for social participation are expanding. Increasing leisure time lies at our disposal. If youth can come to see adequate meaning in life, if it can develop its inner resources and not attach too much importance to the material implements of daily living, it can come to view its prospects with renewed satisfaction.

196

3. Young Americans regard democracy with an attitude, not of skepticism, but of frank questioning. They can see, as can all of us, that democracy is in a measure of distress, and they are led to wonder how serious the complications will turn out to be. Their ideas of just what democracy means are vague and remote from their own day-to-day living. They are likely to think of democracy as a bookish ideal of government rather than as a concrete system of close-at-hand human relationships. They wonder whether democracy can maintain a satisfactory level of economic efficiency; whether it can solve the problem of peacetime unemployment. They hope they will not have to choose between freedom and a decent job. (Heaven forbid that they should have to!) They are impressed with the fact that great inequalities of human circumstances continue to challenge the concept of social justice that lies at the heart of democracy. On every hand they observe a distressing lack of social unity or of any consolidated social purpose. In short, they are troubled about democracy, and despite an underlying belief and loyalty, cannot but wonder what lies ahead.

Let us be thankful that American youth no longer takes democracy in childlike faith. The time has arrived for dealing more openly and constructively with those phases of American life which belie our democratic ideals. After all, democracy is not a blessing conferred for all time on the American people by the Founding Fathers; it is an aspiring purpose to be achieved only as the generations succeed in really establishing peace on earth and good will among men. Eternal vigilance and unending endeavor for its improvement are required for the preservation of democracy. If youth with its frank questioning leads America to replace its complacency toward democracy with honest concern for its future, youth will have served well those democratic purposes for which we all stand.

4. There is much that is essentially fatalistic in the attitude of the American youth toward possible future wars. After all what does youth have to say about whether or not war shall be waged? Youth's job is to fight the war—not to declare it!

As to the causes which provoke wars, American youth is plainly cynical. It is convinced that interests, even more than principles, often prevail, and that popular support for war can be obtained provided those in power have full possession of modernized instruments of propaganda.

American youth is for peace; yet it does not appear to be for "peace at any price." Our young men would be quick to arm if a foreign invasion threatened or if the territorial integrity of continental United States were endangered. But they are not eager to go abroad in defense of democracy.

American youth expects another war and expects the United States to be drawn into it; however, its attitude toward this prospect is not one of willing sacrifice but of fatalistic submission. It is the absence of enthusiasm, the lack of passionate devotion to any cause at all that more sharply than anything else characterizes American youth of this generation. That this is so may well give pause to those of us who are now managing the estate which American youth of these days will in due course inherit.

Early manhood or womanhood is not an easy period of life; it is, in fact, one of life's most difficult periods. Youth needs sympathetic counsel and wise co-operation in working out its problems. I am not one of those who would subordinate adult living to the demands of the oncoming generation; on the contrary, I am convinced that each generation in its prime is entitled to its own time in the saddle. But while there and living in the present, each succeeding generation is under obligation to keep an eye on the future, and the rights and interests of youth—of the generation to come —are to be respected. Youth has its part to play in social planning, and let not its failure to speak be taken as a sign of indifference or complacency. After all, civilizations, like parents, may be judged in part by the thought and care they give to their young.

Note on Sources

"Responsibilities of General Education in a Free Society." From an address at the Fifth Educational Conference, convened by the Educational Records Bureau and the Cooperative Test Service, on October 29, 1936; from an address published in *Vital Speeches of the Day,* vol. X, no. 20 (August 1, 1944); and from "General Education in the Land-Grant Institutions," Ithaca, New York, November 1, 1950.

"Education for Democratic Ideals." From an address given before the National Association of Manufacturers, New York, December 6, 1946.

"Changes in the Organization of American Public Education." From "Oncoming Changes in the Organization of American Public Education," Association of Colleges and Universities of the State of New York, Committee on Teacher Education, May 1941; from a statement at Public Hearings of New York State University Trustees, January 23, 1950; and from an address at the convocation of the University of the State of New York, October 17, 1941.

"Educational Objectives and Teacher Education." From the *Educational Record,* vol. XXII (January 1941), American Council on Education.

"A University and Its Functions." From his inauguration address at Cornell University, October 8, 1937; from *Higher Edu-*

cation in the National Service, a report of a national conference of university and college administrators and educators, government and military officials, and representatives of national organizations, October 6–7, 1950, American Council on Education.

"Education for Practical, Social, and Moral Intelligence." From a commencement address at Michigan State College, June 8, 1946; from a commencement address at Cornell University, June 23, 1946; and from *Educational Forum,* vol. XI, no. 1 (November 1946).

"The Need to Reorient Liberal Education." From an address at the inauguration of Carter Davidson as president of Union College, May 11, 1946.

"Science, Social Progress, and Higher Education." From an address at the annual meeting of the Association of Land-Grant Colleges and Universities, at Chicago, Illinois, November 10, 1941; and from a conference address at Vanderbilt University, March 1–3, 1941.

"Competition between Teaching and Research in American Universities." From a paper read before the Association of American Universities, meeting in Columbus, Missouri, October 30–November 1, 1939, and published in the *Educational Record,* vol. XXI (January 1940).

"Social Responsibilities of Business Education." From a convocation address commemorating the twenty-fifth anniversary of the establishment of the School of Business Administration, University of Michigan, October 5, 1949.

"Education in Industrial and Labor Relations: The School at Cornell." From an address to the New York State CIO convention in 1949 and an article in *Industrial and Labor Relations Review,* vol. 3, no. 2 (January 1950).

"Role of Administration in Higher Education." From an address at the inauguration of James Lewis Morrill as president of the University of Minnesota, April 25, 1946.

"A University President Talks about His Job." From an informal talk at a Cornell University symposium sponsored by the Student Association of the School of Business and Public Administration, February 10, 1949.

"Utilization of Human Resources in a Cold War: The Conant Plan." Ithaca, New York, December 7, 1950.

"Facets of Freedom." From a lecture at the Department of Agriculture, Washington, D.C., April 4, 1942; from a commencement address at Cornell University, June 16, 1947; and from an address to the Economic Club of New York, April 28, 1949.

"Qualities of Democratic Leadership." From an address at the annual luncheon of the Cornell Women's Club of New York, February 5, 1949.

"Of Loyalties." From a commencement address at Cornell University, May 25, 1942.

"A Word on Behalf of American Youth." From an address before the fourth general session of the American Association of School Administrators, February 27, 1939.